T0077871

Victory in Marriage

Biblical Perspective, Christ-Centered Advice, and Real-Life Experience

SARAH NOEL MAXWELL

WESTBOW
PRESS®
A DIVISION OF THOMAS NELSON
& ZONDERVAN

This book is a work of non-fiction. Unless otherwise noted, the author and the publisher
make no explicit guarantees as to the accuracy of the information contained in this book
and in some cases, names of people and places have been altered to protect their privacy.

Some of the anecdotal illustrations in this book are true to life and are included
with the permission of the persons involved. All other illustrations are composites
of real situations, and any resemblance to people living or dead is coincidental.

WestBow Press books may be ordered through booksellers or by contacting:

WestBow Press
A Division of Thomas Nelson & Zondervan
1663 Liberty Drive
Bloomington, IN 47403
www.westbowpress.com
1 (866) 928-1240

Because of the dynamic nature of the Internet, any web addresses or links contained
in this book may have changed since publication and may no longer be valid. The views
expressed in this work are solely those of the author and do not necessarily reflect the
views of the publisher, and the publisher hereby disclaims any responsibility for them.

Any people depicted in stock imagery provided by Thinkstock are models,
and such images are being used for illustrative purposes only.
Certain stock imagery © Thinkstock.

ISBN: 978-1-9736-0518-8 (sc)
ISBN: 978-1-9736-0520-1 (hc)
ISBN: 978-1-9736-0519-5 (e)

Library of Congress Control Number: 2017915000

Print information available on the last page.

WestBow Press rev. date: 9/26/2017

Dedication

To my husband (Preston) for marrying me. If not for that choice to pursue me in 2011 (despite my resistance) and to marry me three years later, I would not know the beauty of marriage or have any credibility to write this book. *Victory in Marriage* and its contents will be something I live by, not just teach by.

With love, your wife, your Love Bug.

Contents

Preface

In July 2015, my husband and I had only been married for just over a year, almost a year and a half. Baby marrieds. In fact, we were long distance for military reasons from February 2014 until May 2015, aside from short trips to be together every few months.

Victory in Marriage started out as an outlet for me, kind of like a journal, to write about things I wished I could talk with Preston at length about but couldn't, or to address what I was feeling in ways that taught me how to be a wife intangibly.

Between graduating college, a short-term job, and a couple of moves, I stopped writing for a while. It wasn't until January 2017 that I picked this up again and decided I have too much to offer you, my beloved readers, to keep for myself. This has become a guide with real experience and honest advice for people of virtually any marital status, especially engaged and newly married couples.

You won't agree with all I say, but I hope you agree with some. I hope—and expect—you will learn some new, insightful things that will challenge you, encourage you, and teach you.

Acknowledgement

To those who helped me polish this book through reading and editing: My Ma and Daddy, Jason and Jenny, and Esther, thank you! I also can't ignore the fact that people (in a different country, no less) took the time to read and endorse my book: Mat and Est, you have blessed me more than you may know! Last but not least, I wouldn't have known the ins and outs of publishing a book at all if it weren't for the support of WestBow Press, specifically Jon Lineback and Venus Gamboa! You answered a lot of questions with grace, clarity, and patience. Thank you so much!

Introduction

My main goal isn't to teach you about having a "happy" marriage, but how to have a "committed" one. Through personal experiences, scripture, and helpful advice from others, you'll get a detailed look inside the messiness of marriage, the work it takes to see it grow, and be exposed to every single emotion known to man!

Prayer, the wedding, money, sex, long-distance relationships, dating, and many other topics will be dissected and hopefully you'll learn something that will equip you to **be the kind of spouse you want to be married to!**

I promise, you'll be encouraged and laugh a bit too!

The heart is the most pulverized, most easily broken, thing in life, and yet is also the toughest organ in the human body (you know, unscientifically speaking). It is the thing associated with love, or lack thereof. It looks better on drawings and notes than on our sleeve or inside our chest. No, this is not one of those books that get hyper-sensitive and mushy gushy (okay, maybe a little). This isn't about the scientific parts of the human heart, either. This is about what our heart does on a more spiritual and emotional level, and how my story has a lot to do with my heart and the hearts of so many others.

My name is Sarah Maxwell. I became a wife on February 22nd, 2014. I am sure it'll have to be a great deal of time before anyone sees me as married "long enough" to give advice on marriage, but really, you can learn a lot about marriage on day one, and even *before* becoming a spouse. My few years married have taught me a lifetime of lessons.

This may be my primary audience, I expect—the people who probably are reading this to perhaps find a marriage victory before their marriage starts. And also, I expect a lot of struggling spouses to be reading this. If you're married and not currently struggling, I'm sure you will still gain insight from this book, so don't leave now…

I will have you know, anything I offer you most likely will not be my own words or thoughts; I don't mean I have plagiarized. Those words will be God's words, and I will offer complementary real-life, personal experience. This may not be so much *advice* as it is *truth*. I think advice has more differing opinions, at times, than it does solid truth.

Truth is what I offer you. I don't think this book should get put on a shelf to collect dust if you *don't* believe in God or the Bible, though, because can't we all learn something valuable from people we disagree with at times? Besides, if someone writes a book to share what they believe is truth, what if it becomes life-changing for you after all? Perhaps the time put into reading *Victory in Marriage* could be worthwhile.

I like to think of this book as more *life-enriching* than *self-help*. In fact, most of what you'll learn is that victory in marriage comes from *others-help*.

I will warn you, if you're like me who sometimes skips book introductions to get to the "juicy" stuff, you likely are not even reading this sentence, but I hope you *do* read this introduction. I truly believe it'll help shape who I am, not just as an author (especially of my first book), but of a *person*—probably a person like YOU. Now, this book is going to focus on marriage and things that precede marriage, go along with marriage, and everything in between.

The making of a beautiful story, one that involves marriage (*my* marriage) started in my 8th grade year. It was in this year that I thought I met "the one" for the very first time. This person, named Justin, was someone I was in a relationship with until senior year of high school. Despite being a teenager, it wasn't just a hold-hands-at-school-and-call-me-girlfriend relationship. It felt true, was communicative and enjoyable, and gave me so many life lessons and challenges. We talked about marriage a lot, mostly after the two-year mark.

Senior year in high school, though, near graduation in fact, something changed. It wasn't as sudden as it felt at the time, though. It was gradual over the course of perhaps the latter two years of the relationship. Time with each other was replaced by time with friends, and our values seemed to contrast more and more. My heart, that organ thing I talked about earlier, started to drift. I believe strongly in it being possible to cheat *emotionally*, or having "affairs of the heart." They may actually hurt worse than physical cheating.

That's what I had...affairs of the heart.

So many factors—my emotional cheating, and his not thinking our spiritual life needed to be talked about— led to a mutual decision between Justin and I that we must end our relationship.

But we need to rewind. Halfway through this relationship with Justin, I was starting my sophomore year in high school. This may have been the most critical point in my walk with Christ, right after asking Him to be Lord of my life at the end of 7th grade. Sophomore year was the year I joined a Christian club at my high school, but not the BIG one where all the Christian athletes were (I am *not* an athlete, by far). This club was about six members that met in miscellaneous places once or twice a week, like the back of the library where Audio-Visual (AV) guys did their work, and in other places like that—unnoticeable. We were a small but mighty group.

That year may have been the best year for my relationship with Justin, too. We both were past the two year mark, which was a serious feat for high school kids who had been together since junior high. But as for Justin's walk with Christ, I to this day am not sure if he had one like I did. Whether he did or not, I know this: God wanted to play matchmaker, but in the right way. Never would God ask me to step away from Justin to *immediately* be with someone more *equally yoked*—at least not without learning who I was in Him first. And know this, God *can* and *does* call people away from relationships if those relationships are unhealthy, but He won't *force us*. Justin and I weren't necessarily in an *unhealthy* relationship, but we knew we were entering a new chapter, one not as a couple anymore. I learned in hindsight that God would place my future husband in the same small Christian Club I was in, because there was a divine time for us to come together years later.

It's like God looked down in my sophomore year with glee thinking *"Oh...just you wait and see, Sarah...you might be in a good place now with Justin, but I've got bigger plans for you down the road..."*

Now, fast-forward again. Two years later, Justin and I had recently broken up, gone to prom with our friends and not each other, and graduated from high school. My future husband, Preston, had gone and had some dramatic life changes occur too, including but not limited to moving to Tennessee to become engaged, and to have that engagement end. Preston was two years ahead of me in high school so this all was happening around the time Justin and I broke up. That ended engagement pushed Preston back to Arizona the *same time* I was healing from the necessary breakup with Justin.

It was no coincidence that my older sister needed help with a computer issue and that Preston knew how to fix it. It was no coincidence that Preston and I started hanging out shortly after that, and that he became my best friend. It was no coincidence that as my best friend—a *male* best friend at that—he stood by me, and bent his ear for me as I cried about the breakup he was acutely aware had happened. Preston fell deeply in love with me.

Don't grab the tissues yet! I didn't fall into his arms ready to marry him yet. In fact, I pushed away any romantic idea I had (which was fairly minimal by then). I didn't even know who I was aside from good grades and having a boyfriend. Now, I didn't even have a boyfriend. I still wasn't *really* focused on God, even though I loved Him and wanted to live for Him. I probably started my habit of worrying here too, and I needed time to figure out who I was. Can you relate? Especially you ladies!

After a while though, I saw Preston every day it seemed, but I started to develop strong feelings for a guy named Thomas. I met Thomas in a very peculiar way on a choir trip I took in New York during my junior year in high school. That trip helped me discover he was on the *same* trip from a *different* school—also in Arizona, where I was living! That was no coincidence either.

Guess what Preston did as he saw me pine for this guy? As Preston fell in love with me and had to watch me pursue Thomas, he didn't actually stop treating me as a friend who he cared for. He didn't even give me an ultimatum—"it's romance or I walk"—like you might expect. Preston probably hung onto me tighter, in fact, and he still bent his ear as I talked about this new possible boyfriend. Now we have a triangle nobody really wants to be in: Preston pursuing me, me pursuing Thomas, and Thomas pursuing football and acting, while still flirting with me! This time in my life may have been one misstep already because honestly, I think the *man* should pursue the *woman* in a Godly way, not the other way around

Before I tell you how this plays out, I must clarify a question some of you might be having. *If she doesn't see any of this as a coincidence, what exactly does she think these incidents all are?* That's easy! My match-maker, my Lord and Savior and God, has orchestrated every event in my life (even before 8th grade) to lead me into a beautiful marriage with Preston. Marriage is not the only beautiful thing God has provided for me; marriage isn't the end all, be all. But marriage and all things God blesses us with tend to start long before we realize they do.

I still didn't *really* want a relationship, but I sort of danced around the idea.

Now for the juicy love triangle story turned hopelessly romantic story....

Thomas moved away, but we have stayed friends. In fact, we support each other in our relationships and can call each other, even after a full year or more, and still speak about our life happenings—and about the more philosophical things like we used to. It's a distant, seldom kind of friendship, but it is still a friendship, and having it any closer would probably be dangerous, given my past "emotional affairs."

Justin—the boyfriend of four and a half years— barely talks with me at all, but through social media I can definitely see that breaking up with each other may have been the catalyst to a life we both are more fulfilled in. The couple times I have seen him have been cordial and decent, and it's a strange contentment seeing him as someone I don't really know anymore.

And Preston, the sweet love of my life, has now given me a taste of my own medicine. As I had Preston follow me through a breakup and that love triangle, I now had to follow him into the United States Air Force. It sounds like a nice twist to the story, but it wasn't. We were now taken into two separate states because I had to finish college in Arizona. I had barely started at the Arizona State University (ASU), actually. Only year one of my relationship with Preston had completed. I knew I was either in it for the long haul, or I had to leave now. But after seeing a young man stand by me through all he had, I knew it'd be near impossible to find someone like that who cared about me like he did. More than that, I loved him very deeply already.

You'll read later on that we were separated by countries at one point, too.

If you've survived this introduction, you're qualified to move forward. If you skipped this, you won't even read this sentence, and I wish you to enjoy *Victory in Marriage* anyway! In all truth, I am just excited you have this in your hands and not on the shelf, so read on! I won't even tell you that you have to read in the order I've written it. God may lead you to a different chapter one day, and that's okay, but this book is written in an order that seems to make everything cohesive, so I challenge you to read all chapters as they are.

Turn down the lamp, turn on the book light, get under the blanket, and hang on with me!

LORD, I pray that whoever has this book in their hands is prepared for some discomfort with a huge dose of truth. Only you can help us receive humility as challenging situations are encountered. A lot can help marriages endure if only we'd understand that marriage isn't about us—and that You are the source of change.

I pray that both spouses are willing to trust You, not just one of them. Marriage can be more beautiful, rewarding, and full of growth than any predictable, sappy modern fairytale because the Author of Life is writing it. You designed marriage. We just have added expensive weddings and a lot of pressure to the thing.

Help us to see you in the days we thought marriage would bring us joy but has appeared to bring us emptiness. You can fill us again. Only You can change our spouse, and change our very self.

Amen/so be it.

1 ❀ Victory Implies Battle

No victory comes without battle.

I FIND IT NECESSARY TO begin this book with a strong defense for our lives being a series of battles—and not some journey to self-happiness. Too often people want victory without a battle, and they want miracles without the pain that comes with *needing* a miracle. This is not to discourage you, but I am not going to lie to you.

Being human, especially being one after God's heart, you will face many trials, and most will be more than you can bear—or at least it will seem that way. Some Christians believe Jesus is a ten-step program to success or riches, or something else very temporary or superficial. But living in the footsteps of Jesus will ask a lot of you and will require serious *discipline* and *discipleship*. I'd rather think that my trials are for God's purpose than for nothing at all.

Some of you may not know Christ—or perhaps you may not even believe in God at all—and your life may be seemingly unchanged by that. Please don't skip this part if that's you! No matter *where* you are or *who* you are, God can meet you! And to those of you hurt by "church people," we are still in a sinful world! Christians have received the Lord and try hard (some of us) to be righteous, but we fail. Both believers and nonbelievers alike seem to think Christians should look as polished as they can, but that is not the true goal. We try to be like Christ not so we can earn His love or a spot in heaven, but because God tells us it'll bring us "life and life to the full" (John 10:10 NIV).

The truth is that we will fall sometimes, and my sin isn't more of an excusable sin than yours or vice versa. The only difference is that we as we follow God *desire not to sin*, and we have God to help us. We all can! The true children of God will seek God in all areas of life, especially *when* they fall. If they are wise, they will seek Him *before* they fall, when temptation hits.

Temptation is not sin; temptation is inevitable. It is just a part of living in a fallen world ruled by the evil one to lure us into giving our souls, our very lives, to eternity in hell—but it's wrapped in the bow of allure to make us desire sin instead of Jesus. You can choose to deny his wiles! Not to be grim, but that is the truth. We cannot follow the Lord, fighting to be like Christ, yet believe there is no evil in this world. More than ever, we experience evil happening around us—and it will get worse. The only difference once we receive the Holy Spirit is the *power* we have against evil now.

James 1:13–18, HCSB says:

> "No one undergoing a trial should say, 'I am being tempted by God.' For God is not tempted by evil, and He Himself doesn't tempt anyone. But each person is tempted when he is drawn away and enticed by his own evil desires. Then after desire has conceived, it gives birth to sin, and when sin is fully grown, it gives birth to death. Don't be deceived, my dearly loved brothers. Every generous act and every perfect gift is from above, coming down from the Father of lights; with Him there is no variation or shadow cast by turning. By His own choice, He gave us a new birth by the message of truth so that we would be the ***first-fruits*** of His creatures."

We will have a lot of trouble in this life. Whether you believe in God or not, we all face it. We have a choice: try to resolve it ourselves, or get help from God—usually through people. Help from God may come in the form of divine intervention, and it may come just as divinely in the form of the human relationships God has placed in your life. Trying to resolve problems on your own may mean you're ignoring the persisting issue, but that is still a fight you are fighting (and likely losing) on your own.

I assure you, none of us are worthy enough, strong enough, or wise enough to defeat all our problems on our own. There are always prices to pay. And you know what? God paid for a lot on that cross, so if you fight on your own, you might be wasting time working hard at a fight that is already won. It doesn't mean you can sit around and expect to see God act on your behalf; it's an active kind of waiting on the Lord, not a passive kind. It means seeking Him and keeping our eyes on Him and His ways, which will keep us in line with the best life here on earth that will prepare us for eternal life in heaven. However, don't misunderstand that having a fulfilling life pursuing God doesn't mean you won't have struggles; in fact, it's a guarantee of them.

It is okay with me if you do not believe all of this, but if I believe in something as truth, I will not keep it secret from anyone, including you, especially not for fear of offending someone. That, like temptations, is inevitable.

Know that you'll have to live through some tough battles to get the victories you want, and you may even have some *lost* battles too; however, losing certain battles may actually cause victories too. For example, it may not be easy to lose friends or family—not to death, but through them shunning or belittling you—when they find out you're one of those "Jesus freaks" now. It may feel like a losing battle, but it will bring victory in many other ways. Trust me, staying true to something—like God being Lord of your life—has a way of showing a light in your life that people notice, and some of them even come to want it themselves. That is a victory.

I must insist that most of our battles are not of the flesh either (even if you are in, or have been in, a war). In fact, most battles we endure will be of the spirit (Ephesians 6:12). The only way to win a battle of the spirit is the same way to win one physically: exercise and train! Stay in God's Word. Pray all the time (it does not only have to be at a meal or before you sleep). Also, follow the steps in the same chapter:

> This is why you must take up the full armor of God, so that you may be able to resist in the evil day, and having prepared everything, to take your stand. Stand, therefore, with truth like a belt around your waist, righteousness_ like armor on your chest, and your feet sandaled with readiness for the gospel of peace. In every situation take the shield of faith, and with it you will be able to extinguish all the flaming arrows of the evil one. Take the helmet of salvation, and the sword of the Spirit, which is God's word. (Ephesians 6:13–17).

Some of my favorite memories, experiences, and feelings involve meeting new people, trying new foods, and singing new songs. Many more of my most genuinely memorable experiences come from a long and terrible trial—and we don't often realize until after the fact that those trials are a blessing. Imagine your child getting lost, or being in a long-distance relationship for a long time, or totaling your vehicle, or whatever you've been through that caused trauma. Now imagine the feeling of finding your child, or of reuniting with your love, or of receiving a new car from your friends that was better than the previous one. Lacking something is necessary so that when we come out of that void with faith in the Lord through persistent prayer, we come out with an "inexpressible and glorious joy" (1 Peter 1:8) and peace "which surpasses every thought" (Philippians 4:7). Our practical needs just might be taken care of too.

My husband and I have been through a few different marriage groups. Counseling and classes aren't just for failing marriages. You can be as strong as ever—at least seemingly—and still gain a lot out of classes and sound advice. They teach you things you wish you knew *before* you got married. I'm going to share some of those tidbits, and trust me, it's only some. I will say that I was, fortunately, told some of these things *before* I married through church, family, or married friends. Trust me, I know not everyone gets that same benefit before they marry.

I am forever thankful that my views of marriage have been wholesome and consistent with those with the strongest marriages.

Marriage is a Covenant, Not a Contract

More than perhaps any other time in the world, we see modern marriage happening for a lot of different reasons, and none of those seem to compare to its original design. We also see marriage being opted out of because people saw their parents get divorced, or they see no difference between married and unmarried people, and so on. I am here to tell you that a lot of people get a wake-up call, and sometimes a divorce, because they realize marriage changes *everything*.

To say that marriage is a *contract* means it can have an escape clause; it means that you can opt out at any time because you have leverage, or have "fallen out of love". It lasts "as long as we both shall *love*," and it is reduced to signing your names on a dotted line—as official as it gets. Marriage as a **covenant**[1] is a solemn oath. If it is broken, it is the most profound way to break a person—well, two people who have become one spiritually. Let's be real, they become one physically too, if you know what I mean! Covenants are based on love and loyalty—the kinds of love and loyalty that endure even when love and loyalty are not reciprocated. It lasts "as long as we both shall *live*," because love is a choice, even when it isn't felt. Yes, you sign names after your ceremony, but it calls for the binding of hearts, which is more official than any document can make marriage to be. Marriage is designed *by* God to *reflect* God's love for His bride, the church.

Sex isn't Pretty

If you'll allow me to be vulnerable, our first week of marriage during our honeymoon was a painful sexual experience. In fact, I couldn't even call it *sex* that soon because it was so…incomplete. It barely started before it ended. But you know what, that was such a short glimmer of our few years married that I barely remember how agonizing it was. Now our love is as full as ever, and completely unhindered. Even now, its beauty does not unfold like it does in the movies. I will address this more later on in the "Honeymoon" chapter, and I can already see several of you trying to skip ahead! This is not 50 *Shades of Grey*, people.

Truly though, sex is meant to be explored, experimental, and enjoyable—with your spouse alone. It's a myth you need to be *experienced* for it to be *exciting*. Just a side note about 50 *Shades of Grey*; watching that honestly can start –or continue—an unhealthy expectation of sex and spiral a porn addict into worse struggles. Don't go there people!

"The One" is a Myth

I will discuss this more in detail later as well, but let me be clear: knowing you want to marry someone, that they are "the one", does not guarantee smooth sailing. Marriages like that don't exist, except in *seasons* of marriage. When people buy into this "the one" myth, they think that just because

---

[1] Covenant: of Latin origin (con venire), meaning "a coming together"

they have disagreements, or dislike their spouse's company at times, that their marriage is a sham, and they need to find a way out. There's that *as long as we both shall <u>love</u>* thing again. Having differences doesn't make you incompatible.

On the same coin, people may think that finding "the one" means marriage will somehow be bliss all days of their lives. That simply isn't true. Of course you'll want to enjoy each other's company and will grow together in every way hopefully, but it takes hard work *after* finding them and marrying them.

Be aware that divorce is biblically discussed, and is permissible in a case or two, but things getting a <u>little uncomfortable</u>, or realizing you <u>don't know your spouse</u> as well as you thought, are absolutely not reasons to call it quits. In fact, those are two aspects of marriage that make it the most mysteriously beautiful thing you'll experience on earth.

In January of 2017, in Family Life's "The Art of Marriage" class, I learned this beautiful metaphor: *"In marriage, like music, two clashing notes create dissonance, which is actually quite beautiful; eventually, though, they need to resolve into harmony."* You two will clash—a lot—and when you can't resolve anything and get to the heart of your feelings, thoughts, and actions, there won't be *harmony*. In music and in marriage, harmony is what gives us relief. Have you ever heard a song not resolve? As a musician, it stresses me to no end because you're left hanging without knowing how it ends. Things need to *resolve*.

My senior friend, David, from a choir I sing in, told me once that "You could potentially be thoroughly happy with every fifth person you meet, but God placed someone specifically in your life, purposefully to be your spouse." This doesn't guarantee a marriage without issues, nor does it mean you'll both love and serve as a spouse without flaw every day, but it does mean that when you find the dents, kinks, and holes in your marriage, you're still with the right person— "the one" as it were.

It's Essential to be Equally Yoked

This is kind of a *Christianese* phrase, so if you are not a *Churched* person or do not know what this means, being *equally yoked* means, in layman's terms, that you both are on the same page. To get right into it—because it's one of the two true deal-breakers to me for getting married—being equally yoked is going to be what helps you *get through* issues, as opposed to *creating* so many more.

As my friend Kathy P. once told me, being unequally yoked "is similar to rowing a boat with one oar." The boat will move a little, and maybe in the direction one of you wants, but the boat wobbles and redirects inevitably. Only one person is working toward a destination; the other spouse couldn't care less if they make it to that particular destination.

You can't marry someone unequally yoked expecting to convert your spouse, or change them in any way, just by being married. It's no guarantee they will ever become a child of God or change a nasty habit by being married to you. We can't change our spouse. All we can do is pray for them and *be* the spouse we want our spouse to be. Marriage is difficult enough in equally yoked situations.

The verse in second Corinthians doesn't say, "Do not be unequally yoked … unless you think the person will change." It says, "Do not be yoked together with unbelievers." (2 Corinthians 6:14, NIV). Period. Will you take that risk? Some people do, and some marriages can survive, and maybe the unbelieving spouse finally believes in God and follows Him after all…but do you want to risk the covenant we just talked about if they *don't*? Again, there are no guarantees. Only God saves, not being married to you.

I know being unequally yoked is *said* to cause issues, but what kind of issues could marrying unequally yoked really elicit? I mean, "he respects my beliefs, so why shouldn't I marry him?" as I often hear. Here are some *possible* issues:

- **You will spend a great deal of time <u>on your own</u>** while you pray, read the Bible, go to church services, help the needy, and so on, and your spouse will consider it a <u>waste of time</u> probably. It'll *be* your life, and it'll feel like a *hindrance* to your spouse.
- Best case scenario is they will <u>tolerate</u> it or maybe even respect it, yet **feel like he/she <u>isn't involved</u> (which will be true), and <u>they likely won't participate with you.</u>**
- **Your spouse may think putting God first means <u>neglecting</u> family,** but following God actually <u>enables us to love our families and friends</u> more deeply and sincerely. Putting God first means putting people *second*, which is<u> still a priority</u> in life.

7

- On a similar note, **the unbelieving spouse won't invite God into every aspect of your marriage**, like through prayer, which is especially detrimental to the husbands who God regards as Head of Household (meaning responsible, protective leader).
- One spouse will *blame* **God for the trials**, and one will *praise* God *through* them and *for* them. **This will make resolving issues nearly impossible.**
- **The unbelieving spouse may not regard marriage as a sacred design** of God and consequently may think <u>divorce</u> is an option if they don't "feel loved", while the believing spouse is in it *regardless of how they feel*.

As you'll read in this book a bit, and experience in real life even more, Satan hates your marriage. Yes, he'll care more to destroy it and cause strife between *you two*, but wouldn't you rather fight the real enemy (the devil) than to fight your spouse because they are unequally yoked with you? Being unequally yoked and the issues they cause can very easily slip you both into divorce or a depressing marriage. There is joy in fighting for your marriage for the sake of becoming more like God with His church—and this applies to equally yoked couples too. You fight on your knees in prayer. You fight by loving and forgiving relentlessly. But again, consider if you want to marry under these conditions if you aren't both *on the same page* with following God together.

As you read earlier, Justin and I broke up because we were unequally yoked, if we're honest. It was ending a good thing to finally get a better thing.

Two deal breakers to ask of your potential spouse before you get married:

1. **Is God the Savior and Lord of your life?** (i.e. do they pray genuinely, spend time in the Bible regularly, and give generously?)… *psst, this is what we just talked about, with being equally yoked, and it's not just "going to church."*
2. **Do they want to start a family?** Whether it is "yes" or "no," I consider this one something you **must** be on the same page about. Some people get married *so they can start a family!* If one spouse doesn't want a family, it doesn't mean getting married to them will change their mind.

Other issues like money management, discipline styles, and many other items are important to discuss, but aren't necessarily deal breakers.

Fighting, Even When Equally Yoked

You will fight, but fight fair. It's a myth to think when you marry someone you're in love with that you won't fight, or that fighting makes them less "compatible." Ask any Godly married couple you know, and see just how *different, opposite,* and seemingly *incompatible* they actually are! **Don't threaten anything**—especially divorce, or bodily harm on yourself, your spouse, child, or anyone. And **listen.** Listen to *understand* not to *respond* (trust me, I know it's a tough one, especially when you're sure you're right!). Give them **eye contact.** Sit down, make a coffee, and *listen* (yes, I meant to put that twice). **Hold hands** when you talk; don't make fists or cross your arms. Turn a stressful issue into a meaningful opportunity to understand each other.

You may not really *like* your spouse one day, but pause and consider what situation you're in and how it could be straining you or your spouse. You can still *love* them when you don't *like* them much. When my husband and I had to go on some military training trip for half a year or so, away from the comfort of our new house back home, he was usually more stressed out and irritable (most like how I am on *normal* days), so I had to give him *more* grace, not *less.*

One of the ways you're probably opposite is one of you likes to resolve issues *now,* and one likes to process and think on it so they can resolve it *later.* Communicate a time to resolve the issue if it isn't immediately; don't leave it hanging for the one who wants to address it now. Between Preston and I, I'm the one who wants to resolve things the first second possible. He prefers to sit on it for a while, formulate some thoughts and solutions before spilling it all on me. Both ways have their risks and benefits.

For some fights or discussions, you may need to resolve something then and there, and for some others you may have to say (or hear) "I need to think about this for [X amount of time]; let's reconvene then." Usually my husband needs an hour or two. One of you may need a full day. But I wouldn't go too long because letting things sit too long on the backburner eventually boils over. And I must reiterate that it basically torments the spouse who likes to deal with things *now* to have to wait, and it is worse tenfold when they don't know *when* you'll sit down and settle a matter. The key is to not leave either one of you guessing. You both need to share how you feel, why you feel that way, how to address those feelings, and only at the time you both agree to discuss it all.

Addressing feelings usually get messy when spouses don't make clear what they want.

-   Do you need advice?
-   Do you need an ear to bend?
-   Do you need a hug in silence?

Whatever it is, tell your spouse. If you're unsure what your spouse needs, *ask*.

Also know that some *small annoyances* are worth dropping before it becomes a *big fight*. Almost always there is a deeper issue; bigger arguments often bring out the tiny, seemingly insignificant fights from the past. It takes some stupid arguments and discernment to figure out what is worth dropping and what is worth addressing. Sometimes, too, addressing an issue involves you and the Lord. Some matters resolve after some old fashioned prayer—usually more than one.

One day in February of 2017, I got annoyed with a wrong address on my online church profile; even after I edited it, it stayed the same old address. It was a minor technological issue that may not even have affected anything for several months— if at all. (Eventually it did get resolved by the way). In response to my complaining, my husband said I stress too easily and it doesn't help anything; I felt attacked and I wanted his comfort, even if it *was* a small issue that wouldn't disturb *him*; even if he was right. He couldn't fix it, but I didn't need a fix. Before I finished explaining this to him, he plugged in his headphones. It felt as though a matter so petty was not worth his time to listen even one minute longer.

How could I come to him with things of more importance in the future if I worry he won't find it important enough to listen, that he might pick and choose what is worth his time listening to?

Of course, when he plugged in the headphones, I walked away hurt and angry, satisfying his wish for me to leave him—and the issue—alone.

When we discussed it later that night, he told me both that I was "blabbing on" and that he was waiting for me come to him to continue discussing it later. I got upset again because me "blabbing on" was a direct message from his wife telling him exactly what I needed, leaving him no guessing, which men usually want! But he shutting me out mid-sentence with his headphones told me he was *done* discussing, so how could he expect me to come to him later? I'd *like* to discuss the issue immediately, but he closed the door on it before I was done talking…and he wants me to assume he is ready later?

For those of you, likely ladies, who are reading this, shaking your head at my husband, know that he was under a lot of stress that particular day himself, and I *was* over-reacting about something small. In the end, though, *his* actions and tone of voice upset me far worse than a wrong address online. When you do start to talk about anything of even slight importance, talk about *you* and *your* feelings and thoughts, not *your spouse* and what *they did wrong. Not first anyway.* They'll want to share their piece too, and you need to *listen* like I shared above. You'll hit the deeper issue—usually a communication error or some unresolved hurt feeling from the past—and may not even need to deal with the *surface* issue (the wrong address) which ignited the deeper one.

Marriage isn't Private

I do *not* mean to say marriage isn't intimate nor that every sore spot should be put on display, although vulnerability can provide for honest support. I *do* mean that married people should cling closely to *other* married people of God as closely as they cling to each other as spouses.

I can't respond better than my married friends did here, so I will share some insights they responded with when asked what they wish they knew prior to marriage.

I discussed this with my own husband, and he said:

> "When it comes to the subject of what I wish I knew before marriage, it is not something I took lightly. I as a person don't make any life-changing moves without much consideration and thought. I had so many aspects to weigh,

but to know that I was entering into a union that <u>affected not only me</u>, but an amazing lady, which I could share so much of my love with, was inspiring. . . . When you enter into the marriage <u>covenant, your walk with God must be firm.</u> Your religious practices, seeing as <u>your marriage is founded on Christ</u>, must be in place. Mentally, to come to terms that <u>your dating days are over</u>. You have found your "fish of the sea" for <u>the rest of your life</u>. Now you must turn to devote your time, attention, love, respect, finances, and thoughts to your spouse, <u>who also chose you</u>, to LOVE you <u>unconditionally</u> and for eternity."

Because I know my husband more than any other person I know—maybe even myself—I know his intention behind everything he said, and I have the luxury of discussing things way more at length with him than with anyone else. I want to address some of his thoughtful points so he is adequately portrayed.

When Preston talks about "religious practices," he is not limiting the *relationship with God* as only a religious practice, which in turn inspires our marriage relationship; in fact, it's his most sincere acknowledgement of following God being as much a *lifestyle* as religions tend to be. Having grown up Catholic, which probably identifies itself as a religion more than anything, it is part of his vocabulary, and "religion" to him goes much deeper than it means to most other people. Know that he and I don't consider ourselves *converted to a religion*, but *transformed by a growing, challenging, and rewarding relationship with God*.

Also, when he says "your dating days are over," he means *with other people*. Trust me, the dating *of each other* has only gotten better and more frequent than before marriage (frequent doesn't have to be daily, but it should be *consistent*).

My friend AnnaMarie had two very important points regarding what she wished she knew:

"The first thing that comes to my mind is that <u>the struggle is [part of] God's will in marriage, not the absence of struggles</u>, for in the struggle they both become better.

Iron sharpens iron. Many times marriage can be the most tempestuous place on earth and that is not a bad thing; it means that people are changing and opportunities are granted to make that happen. God puts people together not because they are alike and can get along perfectly the way they are but so they can help each other get better. That is why opposites attract. God planned it that way. . .

. . . Another thing that was a revelation to me sometime after I got married was that <u>it is sometimes unromantic, and it does not diminish the beauty or strength of a marriage to compromise or make trade deals.</u> . . . I used to think that if he loved me he would automatically want to do whatever I ask him or whatever is important to me. That is a lie. <u>Love does not make a person all of a sudden enjoy something that is not enjoyable to them.</u> But compromise and trade deals can negotiate us through those tough spots in a glorious way."

An acquaintance of mine, and mother of these two baby twins I used to care for, said this about marriage:

"<u>Marriage is not 50/50</u>. Most of the time one partner needs to be stronger than the other . . . sometimes you are both down and you wrap your arms around each other and <u>weather the storm together</u>." Hilary W.

Such truth to that. Each partner should always aim to give and love 100%. But when you're sick, healing, mourning, or other trials come, it may not be 100% for one of you, or even both of you. The point is that you don't do the bare minimum and hope your spouse feels adequately as precious as God saw them when He gave them to you.

My husband's friend TJ had something short and sweet to share, and it is basically the truest and most exciting statement ever:

"The first year isn't always the best. For some it's the most challenging."

He has wisdom here. This is good news! We can look forward to something better than the "honeymoon phase." The first year you might feel invincible, even if you're broke financially, and "breaking in" each other in every way, but it doesn't take long to take some hits. If you are a married couple where *both of you* follow God, Satan has a target on you both because he hates marriage. He hates what it symbolizes with God and the Church, and he hates that two people of God are that much mightier together.

It's this strange thing: I love my husband *fully* (when I am at my best anyway), yet somehow every passing year, the amount of my love *fills higher*, like the brim of our love increases with time. It's like somehow God calls me to a higher standard of sacrificial love than what my highest was previously. There's something special about learning about someone deeper, knowing them longer, loving them wider. Imagine what it will feel like when you're married fifty years, sixty years! That's a lifetime!

This is not a comprehensive list, nor is this going to fix you up to have a flawless marriage. We are simply giving you fair warning: you'll see your spouse's ugly side.

Satan will try to destroy your marriage as it strengthens.

My friend Steve, who married his wife Kristin a month before Preston and I married, said half-jokingly, "I wish I knew about the giggling in her sleep!" He continued, "but in seriousness, it isn't necessarily what I 'wasn't expecting,' but [rather] just realizing more how much I want to be 'for her'. I was married before, and that spouse was molested before, and in our about eight years of marriage, it would have been nice to know how it would affect our marriage...I didn't even know until the marriage was over!"

Along similar lines, Steve's wife Kristin said "I wish I knew how selfish I was, and what an adjustment it was to change from 'me' to 'us.' I have to remember to confer with Steve about many things, and he defers to me too. Also, Steve has been immersed in God's Word, and has lived it out from a young age, and it has been a HUGE benefit in our marriage."

I know just how much she means this because despite being one of the brightest lights for Jesus that I know, she hasn't followed God long—not even as long as me, and she has more years of life under her belt than I do. To so immediately see how a Godly husband has benefited her walk is a blessing. They both have blessed *each other*, truly.

When speaking to my mom and dad about what they wish they knew before marriage, my mom said that "as changes happen—be it sickness, having kids, job changes, etc.—you're not just going through something singularly. <u>Two people are going through every change</u>, and at different speeds and in different ways too."

You have to be able to navigate through every problem and even every victory, along with learning about how to get through it as <u>a unit</u> now. My dad said he wish he knew that his health would "go south so early in life. It has made me miss a lot in your kids' life." Ever since I was in elementary school, or sooner, I remember my dad telling me he would have to stop working. I have seen the degenerative arthritis in his back branch out into other issues with certain organs and his overall health.

That's the "in sickness" part of your vows. It's not just about making chicken noodle soup when your spouse has a cold. It's years of my mom working more when my dad stopped; it's her sorting his daily meds so he doesn't take too many by mistake because of the crazy symptoms he has experienced, like forgetfulness; it's grace when help doesn't happen around the house as often anymore because it's too painful for him to stand.

Love is my dad working 3 jobs literally around the clock when my mom had 4 children under age 5 at home. Sometimes, love isn't fun or all that love-story-worthy. But it's worth it because of how much you have to pursue it, much like Preston getting the reward to marry me because he pursued me gently.

When talking with my friends Jason and Jenny, one of the strongest, most enduring marriage examples I have ever seen, Jenny told me that "[marriage] . . . is really hard. You'll often be <u>disappointed and hurt</u>. You'll need to <u>pray for your spouse so often</u>! Sometimes it's not till you're married and difficult things happen that the icky parts come out and <u>you realize who you married</u>." Now Jenny and her husband Jason, in their first eight or so years of marriage, really had an astronomically difficult time enjoying their marriage, let alone feeling married at all.

The spiritual warfare that surrounded their marriage, especially Jason, is amazing. Basically every vow you could have broken, or every trial you could have gone through, they went through. Out of sensitivity to the complexity of their past, I won't go into detail. What's more is this: to know Jason *as he is* after that long spiritual war that God brought him through is a testament to a committed marriage, even when it was one-sided for so long. Jason is too humble to ever accept this compliment, but Jason is as close to Jesus Christ as any human being could ever be. Jason elaborated on marriage for him:

> "I wish I would have known how to be more <u>sensitive to my wife's needs</u> and been more <u>selfless</u> . . . I wish I would have been <u>quick to forgive</u> any and every wrong and not taken things she said the wrong way. I wish I would have spent more time <u>reading God's Word with her and in prayer with her</u> to draw us closer to Jesus and to each other. I wish I would have <u>seen myself through Jesus' eyes and known my worth in Christ</u> so I would have spent more <u>quality time</u> with her and not been afraid to <u>pursue her intimately.</u> I wish I would have <u>not been afraid of rejection</u> and just pursued her frequently.
>
> I wish I would have known <u>how to receive God's love and forgiveness right away</u> so I would be able to <u>give it generously to my wife</u> and be more of a <u>joyful man of God to be around</u>. I wish I would have learned how to <u>let go of the past and just be able to really enjoy the good things that God has given me.</u> I wish I would have not been so <u>afraid of failing</u> and just <u>stepped out in faith in Jesus' name</u> more often. I wish I would have <u>taken the initiative</u> as a man more often. I wish I would have <u>known God's grace sooner</u> and <u>His perfect love</u> for me so I could <u>shower my wife in it.</u>
>
> I wish I would have known the <u>power of words</u> sooner- the damage and consequences of tearing down and complaining, and the rewards and benefits of building her up in Christ and speaking God's Word over her and telling her who she is in Christ and what a blessing she's always

been to me. I wish I would have <u>been more thankful</u> for her and <u>more kind</u> all the time like my Savior, Jesus Christ. I'm sure I could think of plenty more things I wish I would have known to <u>make her know she's loved and valued</u>. <u>*I just want to be more like Jesus and be ever so faithful to Jenny always, every day, in every way.*</u>"

This is a long list of wishes, but to see their marriage and to say it's perhaps the most Godly, wholesome, fun marriage I know is a testament to God's hand of grace and how much God can restore broken marriages. It was difficult too, to say the least. Jenny could have rightfully ended the marriage but God said to wait it out. He gave this marriage victory after victory.

Love comes with pain. Most vows say that very thing.

Marriage is undoubtedly the most wonderful and wild, scary and sensual, exhausting and exhilarating ride. Sometimes it can even feel like waiting in a stupidly long line to even *get married*, right ladies? Then when you get there, you barely have enough time to put on your seatbelt before you plummet down a crazy drop! Jenny was essential to keeping me accountable as an almost-married woman. She joked that Jesus would come back and rapture us before I got to experience my honeymoon.

So thankful that didn't happen!

Jesus, I pray against the tactics of evil. Evil is Satan's home, and we experience his unwelcomed presence in so many aspects of our (future) marriages that we are tempted to see marriage as not worth it... We need You around the clock, not only to be the spouse we want our spouse to be, but to fight the right way, on our knees in prayer.

Amen/so be it.

2 ❀ Dating

*Romance: beautifully sacrificial; beyond words and
explanation; misunderstood; a sickening longing for (and
welcoming reception of) freedom, beauty, truth, and love.*

DON'T WANT TO BURST your bubble and say there is no romance in
the world and relationships, but I don't want to lie to you and say that
without a little money, effort, and selfless decisions you can achieve *happily
ever after—even when you have unhappy days.* I most certainly will not tell
you that you should be in a relationship to "be happy" either. Happiness is
not the goal of marriage, or of life, or of following God; it can at best be *a
part of it all,* but the goal is much more self-sacrificing and permanent.

First of all, happiness is an emotion that we forfeit when we suffer
losing a loved one to death, when someone hurts us emotionally, when we
stub our toe, when we buy a damaged item, and so on. There is no way we
can at some point be happy the rest of our lives without also experiencing
all other emotions at some point.

You'll notice I will parallel marriage and courtship, or the dating period,
to relationship with God, with Jesus. So I'll make this connection: I don't
think we can be *happy* forevermore while walking with Christ. Sure, God
will change our lives if we let Him and will offer us pure *joy* even when
trials come, but we grow up learning the weird and inaccurate we-need-to-
make-God-happy thing, and that accepting Him into our heart will make
us happy. But happiness doesn't last. It comes in waves.

But let's talk about **joy** for a second. Joy, at least to me, is the choice, and
sometimes the associated feeling, of gratitude and contentment *even when*
your life is falling apart. Even when you aren't *happy,* you can have *joy.* In

scripture, joy is a fruit of the Spirit (Galatians 5:22) and is experienced in overwhelming ways. It is more permanent than happiness.

How the World Does Dating

Let me address a misconception. That is, in the world, dating seems to be something like interviewing, where everyone puts on their best clothes and best faces with their best stories. You know, where you take a weakness and make it sound like a strength, so later into things they'd look a fool to back out now, right? Usually, two people meet somewhere at a designated time and place, prepared with personal anecdotes and questions for the other person, trying to figure out where they are going with each other, where they stand, what their next steps are.

Sure, that doesn't sound that bad, except for some **eustress,** and sometimes even *distress,* prior to it all. But, why is there confusion? Why does there have to be any question where they are going, where they stand, what their next steps are? Don't get me wrong; be careful and wise and patient if you fervently want to marry. All I'm saying is once the "interview" is over, and you're in a relationship that is "Facebook official," what's different? Is dating the chance to live in the same place together and perhaps do physical, sexual things together? That's how the world seems to treat dating.

Let's be honest, it isn't common to marry the first person we date, so why give it all to the first decent person you date?

Being in *friendship* with people—the hanging out in a group, probably with other God-followers, and with good food and lots of conversation—is how you get to know people the most, and it isn't as stressful as dating the way the world does it. If you feel helpless in the friend-zone, know that I friend-zoned the man who patiently (but actively) pursued me and is now my husband!

Let me tell you just how dating *could* be, especially if you are in it to potentially find a spouse—in no rushed amount of time, of course.

Engaged and Living Together. I get it, we are in a modern age, and I don't necessarily think you'll be condemned to hell if you are living together or did live together before you married...I am definitely not in a place to ever judge someone who wants to be around someone they love, and to perhaps save money by consolidating under one roof.

But I want to explain why my husband and I did <u>not</u> live together, and also why I think it's the better choice—or at least a choice to consider.

Let's get real first. Most people want to live together because they want to experience marriage-like things, like sex. If you don't believe it matters that you save your *first time* for your wedding night, then I cannot expect you to ever understand, agree, or abide by this.

For my husband and I, the most influential reason for NOT living together was because we would be extremely attracted to each other and our will was only so strong people! Even just being around each other for mere hours, especially if we were only with each other and no other friends or family at the same time, made it perfectly dangerous. We knew that living together would not be wise. We knew better, and staying over even for a few nights would absolutely push us into sin. For us, we believe premarital sex is sin, and at the very least a delicate matter in general.

He and I never had sex *with each other* before marriage, but we definitely struggled with the temptation. He isn't a virgin, so he experienced it all before even meeting me. I would argue, though, that it wasn't as beautiful and exquisite as God created sex to be because he was, in a way, reading something out of context. Despite sex being emotional and an act of love on his part, sex wasn't *sacred* for him. We don't believe in saving that sacred first time just because "the Bible says so," but because of marriage itself.

We believe God designed marriage **not** to be a contract with escape clauses and government papers. By contrast, a *covenant*, meaning divine commitment, if you break it, is similar to literally cutting something whole in half. This is always painful, or at least cannot be restored without serious intervention. Since we believe this about marriage, we take the celebration of marriage to involve the wonderful, messy, novel experience of sex. Sex is to be for married people, because what then will be the biggest difference or reward when you're married if you steal that experience beforehand? Once you live like you're married, you may say "eh...no need to marry now." But that tells me you see it as more of a governmental contract than a heavenly covenant, or just some show in the form of a wedding for your loved ones.

Contracts and official papers are still important mind you, but marriage on principle is far more important.

How many of us married the first person we thought we would marry? I didn't. I married the RIGHT person, but I really thought at least once or twice I would marry someone else, before I even dated my husband! Too many people thought they would marry person A, had sex with them, and even had a child or many children with them, and didn't end up marrying after all. In the end, that's stealing from that person's future spouse, and yours. Best case scenario is you're acting married, but are deciding not to *actually* marry—rendering it either not as sacred as God designed it, or just some formality to be disregarded because "it's just a piece of paper."

Sex isn't just a physical activity; it might, in fact, be the only enjoyable part of life that involves every sense and every part of you—your body, yes, but also your heart, mind, and spirit. If you give all of that to someone and never marry, you'll do more damage to your heart, mind, and spirit (and theirs) than you may ever see. It's like tricking those parts of you that you're married, like God planned it, but since you are not, you walk away and break apart painfully, like two hearts being ripped from the chest. For some people who have sex with many people before marriage, they keep experiencing that over and over again.

Even those who have one-night stands or casual sex with people and say "it was only physical" really have a limited understanding of the sexual relationship between people.

Now, the second reason we didn't live together was it actually wasn't financially possible or physically possible. Preston lived with his mom for a while, then with some friends, then in dorms on the base *in a different state than me*, and I was with my parents all the way through college.

Now here's the thing, it might be more practical, more convenient, and more enjoyable living with someone you really love and expect to marry anyway, but ask yourself: what will your marriage be like? It won't always be convenient, practical, or even enjoyable at every moment. Is this person worth saving your body for? Are they worth preparing your heart, mind, and soul for this commitment? You don't need to "test run" the sex or the living together like some car you're going to buy; this is a person, and you'll either stick to your vows or you won't. Marriage is a fight with many difficult choices and emotions—two-fold because it involves two people, their families, and more if you have children.

This may not be for the people who are not following the Lord, but if you are following the Lord, is your spouse worth the wait? ...even when it's hard, or when it doesn't make full sense, or even when you've already had sex, like my husband did before me? That's the hard one for most people; once they've tasted it, it's difficult to stop, and some people say it's too late to start over, but it isn't. It's just a choice you make. One of Preston's largest testaments of love for me was his willingness to fight and wait for that with me after he had experienced it with other women, and we were engaged a year and a half! It had to have been torturous! If we were not long distance we probably would have fallen into that seductive trap and had sex before marriage. I might have even decided to just live with him and forget the struggle of it all...

How long should you be engaged? I am no expert or anything, but as long or as little as you need to be. You don't need to be rich or have a huge house to marry. It really just comes down your hearts. I am *not* saying that both of you being unemployed is a perfect platform for marriage, and money wisdom is really important in marriage, but becoming married doesn't make you automatically better off financially, nor does being wealthy guarantee a flawless marriage.

Do you understand –and agree on—what commitment marriage will require? Do you understand your spouse's expectations? Have you gone through some sort of premarital counseling or classes? It never hurts to try it. People, often men, struggle with the idea of letting *anyone else* tell them what's wrong in their (future) marriage and how to fix something they want to fix on their own, but that's not all these classes are about. They can be eye-opening. It is a chance to learn things from married people about things you really want to know as you enter your marriage! Things like money languages, love languages, communication tools, personality differences, respect versus love, are topics that get dissected.

My husband said once, "if you had let me have sex with you [before marriage], it would just be like any other time, and getting married it would be no different, and it wouldn't be new. There would be no reward—not just making love, but the reward of making love *with you*." Men can be men and still be honorable. In fact, my definition of manhood requires honor.

If you can't afford to live on your own, can you live with your parents, or same sex friends, to split rent? My parents didn't even require I pay rent at all! How about save for your marriage that way, instead of cheating your marriage out of the newness it is supposed to be. Consider your true intentions and take time to be sure about marrying this person before you consolidate assets and cohabitate.

How Dating Should Be and Can Be

I am going to give you two scenarios, and I want you to think about which you would prefer. These are not the only two scenarios that could happen in anyone's dating life, but they are common—perhaps the most common. These are fictional, but very realistic.

Scenario 1

I am 20 years old and have had a few relationships, if you could call them that. I mean, I called this guy my boyfriend but we were only dating for a few weeks, and I barely saw him because we went to different colleges. I've been lonely so I have looked at every online dating website and app I can think of, and even went out with a few people. I am with one of those guys now, but he seems to be only into being physical with me, and doesn't seem to want to marry me someday. I don't even know if he wants a family someday. Anytime I mention kids he skirts around the subject and talks about something else.

He is a nice guy I suppose, but we are on different pages it seems. I haven't talked with him about marriage heavily or anything, but I can tell he wants to see me a lot, but not to eventually marry... even the idea of living together scares him. I like him though. I even found him on a Christian dating site, but I am pretty sure he doesn't even have a relationship with the Lord. He just goes to church because his parents did and I guess that's okay, right? But what man after God pursues my body more than my heart?

Scenario 2

Have you ever felt like you've been single so long, you think you might always be single? Well, some days I feel that way. But other days, I have more hope. There's this guy…I've known him since I was in high school and I've already graduated from a university. We are very close friends. We aren't in a relationship or anything, but we both actually go to some church events together. In fact, I don't see him much outside of those groups and events. I've tried to hang out with him, just him and I, but he always convinces me to make it with at least two other people. But there are those moments, when we are out with mutual friends, that he and I capture a glance at each other, and my heart practically bounces out of my chest. His eyes alone are charming, but it isn't just about that...he looks into my own eyes when we talk. He responds directly to what I've said. He asks if I want advice or prefer to just have him listen when I come to him sad or upset. I don't know what it is, but something is there. I feel it. I think he does too. And we are only just friends...for now, I hope!

❧

Notice that in scenario one, there was a boyfriend-girlfriend thing going on, but it was shallow and uncertain and not a full image of a relationship worth having. Even friendships should be deeper. In fact, friendships are what make romantic relationships possible. It doesn't sound true, but it is. Friends are people you see and talk to sometimes more than family, and you know your family very well, likely. If someone wants to be more than just friends with you but is denied that—you know, being "friend-zoned"—it can seem like complete rejection, but my husband experienced friend-zoning from me, and now we are married. He just had to endure being in my life, however that looked. For us, it was being "just friends" for quite a while first!

In scenario two, there was something mysterious and patient about a bond between two people, and they were just friends—friends who were very attracted to each other, and remained honorable. I wouldn't be surprised if some of my readers desired scenario one, just to have *someone* as a companion, or to be that rocky first boyfriend or girlfriend that everyone seems to have, but I also wouldn't be surprised if they are not transformed by the love of God either.

Let's be honest, the world has a very hopeless, tiring, and rushed way of dating. On top of that, a lot of the world has been hurt by church people, or are deceived into thinking they can never be good enough to have a relationship with God, or that they are not smart enough to study the Bible (where I gauge my whole life's decisions, personally). Being so insecure about God and purpose can hugely affect perspectives in dating. You settle for mediocrity when just a bit of patience and discipline could provide you with much more depth.

I believe relationships with people—romantic and not—and the success they have or don't have, relate very closely to if we have a relationship with Jesus Christ.

Think about those two scenarios. Which one would make you want to get to know someone more? Which one would make you feel most valued? Which ones leaves you most worried and insecure? Which one would you actually want to have? Which one would result in marriage?

Maybe you already know you're in one of those scenarios.

Savior, we need more saving. We praise you for rescuing us from the penalty sin required, but we still need You to save us: from a selfish marriage, or from temptations outside marriage, or from misconceptions about dating that have infiltrated how we interact with our (future) spouse. For those with children who are learning about dating from scary places, I pray that their parents can be the loudest voice telling them what dating can be—not pressure-filled, physically-inappropriate self-selling, but a precious, emotionally intimate friendship that transforms into two people desiring to be one flesh, a unified unit pursuing You in (and prior to) marriage.

Amen/so be it.

3 ❧ Purity

Love: <u>living</u> dreams you <u>do</u> share with someone and <u>supporting</u> the dreams you <u>don't</u> share; daily weeding out the fear, struggles, and temptations; patiently letting God (love in its purest form) lead the way, HIS way.

The Definition

THE DEFINITION OF PURITY, according to a Google© search, is *freedom from adulteration or contamination; freedom from immorality, especially of a sexual nature.* Doesn't that sound ideal? What exactly contaminates? Freedom from immorality...could that happen? What if I already had sex and I'm not married?

These are real questions with real answers. They just probably aren't the easy ones. They are pretty *simple*, though.

Before we get into what is acceptable before marriage and some types of purity to consider, let's look at what scripture has to say.

1 Corinthians 6:18 (HCSB) says:

> "Flee from sexual immorality. 'Every other sin a person commits is outside the body', but the sexually immoral person sins against his own body."

Okay, so...what is sexual immorality? What if I don't have sex, but do some things? I'd have to tell you that if it is even a question, you should avoid it. People in the world tend to date and automatically start to get more physically intimate. You don't have to actually have sex to be sexually immoral. A lot is inappropriate if not married, and we will look into that later.

1 Thessalonians 4:5 (NIV) talks of abstaining from "passionate lust," and if we are honest, we know when we are consumed with lust. It usually takes over every thought and distracts from everything else; lustful thoughts may also lead to lustful *actions* without second thought.

Types of Purity

Physical. "Marriage must be respected by all, and the marriage bed kept undefiled, because God will judge immoral people and adulterers." (Hebrews 13:4).

Imagine being in a relationship with someone for a long time. You start longing to be sexually intimate with them, just like you're emotionally intimate in your late night conversations. And imagine that you both let your walls down and give in after a short fight of resistance, and something happens in one or both of your hearts long after that incident which leads you to break up—maybe the sense of shame or guilt, or something unrelated. It happens. And now, that person has a part of you that cannot be given back—not just physically, but mentally, emotionally, and spiritually. It sounds cliché, but your future spouse will not get to have you quite like they would have if you had understood just what was at stake and waited. Even if that spouse turns out to be the same person you fell with!

This is not to make you feel guilty. God created us to be connected this deeply. It's a myth that sex is bad[2]. Even for people who shamelessly have one-night stands and casual sexual relationships, it involves all parts of their being, but they don't realize the pieces of themselves they sacrifice every time they throw it away for moments of pleasure.

Part of me doesn't want to be too harsh, but the other part of me knows that I have to leave no questions, and leave the sugar-coating behind, because even small tastes of the whole "pie" leave me questioning what I believe,

---

[2] For more information on how men (and women) are wired and how this sex-saturated culture has made it very difficult for marriages to resist temptation, and how to counteract misconceptions about men's visual nature, see the books listed in the Bibliography section at the end of this book. Shaunti Feldhahn's *For Women Only* and *For Men Only* are really helpful and easy reads—okay, easy in language, difficult in practice.

wondering if I am doing the wrong thing, and asking what I'd miss on my wedding night.

Mental, Emotional, and Spiritual. "Create in me a clean heart, O God, and renew a right spirit within me." (Psalm 51:10, NIV).

Creating a clean heart, which only God can do, is half the battle of staying *physically* pure. If you have already experienced or exploited your physical sexual nature, you know you can't exactly go back—physically anyway. Mentally and spiritually— oh my goodness!—you can always start over!

But your emotions, your heart, may see the consequences of not waiting to have sex in marriage way down the road. If you want to avoid some of that, disciplining yourself to wait is the only way, but that leads to the question of what *is appropriate* outside of marriage.

I admire people who have never kissed anyone ever until they are at the altar with their soon-to-be-spouse. Their first kiss is one that starts their marriage. However, I definitely kissed, and then some, before marriage. I hadn't done it all, praise the Lord, but I have done too much. I had kissed guys, and kissing led to a lot more, and not just with the man I ended up marrying.

My own husband had not waited until marriage to be with women sexually, so I had a hard time reconciling the unforgiveness and resentment I had. Sometimes the emotional toll of having sex before marriage reveals itself to your future spouse, not to yourself. If you have never had sex, consider your future spouse's feelings before you do. Is waiting until marriage, being very different from most of the world, that much to ask? I'm not asking if it's difficult. It's torturous! How much are you willing to sacrifice for someone you love that deeply, or *will* love that deeply? Animals react bodily; we don't have to. Men and women are worth way too much to defile something so sacred. What a testament to be so different than most of the world!

Can you kiss before marriage? Honestly, you need to be honest about that with the Lord. It's not a sin to kiss necessarily. Could it cause temptation? Likely. Holding hands and kissing cheeks tend to be more delicate and innocent, so only you and your future spouse can know what the limit is with those things, but less is definitely more in building anticipation of that first wedding night.

I must point out something that, in my opinion, will without fail lead you to premarital sex: living together. I know how much you want to "trial run" the living in the same place every day thing, but if you are in the same house, sharing the same bed, or even rooms that are next to each other, and sharing showers and getting to know someone that closely, what do you think will happen? Instead of a neighborhood or a city separating you, you've got a bedroom or maybe not even that much. And you may start at "just kissing," but trust me, it never just stops there. I give you maybe two weeks—in most cases—before you start toying with the idea that you can "just have sex" because you're "getting married soon anyway."

Need I remind you that we were *created in every way* to enjoy a lot more than kissing? It is inevitable. Sex is good! Although sexual affection is so good, it requires extreme care when handled; it needs to be seriously prepared for. I know people who *don't* live together have had premarital sex too, but how much greater is the chance when you share a home—probably a tightly spaced first apartment?

Take my word for it, if you want to be pure on your wedding night: read scripture on this subject and pray, asking God to give you the desire to remain pure, and date your future spouse in the comfort of Godly groups of people. Start now. Practice diligent waiting so when your first night comes as a married couple, you really are an unopened gift.

If you are engaged or have been together with someone for a long time, don't have sex with them prematurely just because you know you will get married. How much does marriage mean to you if you can't even wait until then? Again, I might be sounding harsh. I realize how deeply you must desire your future spouse! I know marriage likely means a great deal if you're considering marriage at all—I don't mean to imply otherwise— but we either want to prepare to be a Godly spouse even before marriage, or we pick and choose what we will obey.

IT WILL NOT BE EASY! You will want to get around this and will be tempted beyond measure, because the devil hates marriage and will do everything he can to mess up the newness of it before it begins. The biggest fight against Satan is to tell him he cannot have your marriage!

Pornography, the New Drug

Don't believe the lie porn sells to you. Porn demonstrates abusive power of our bodies and diminishes the intentions of what sex can beautifully be within marriage. We weren't meant to watch others have sex, or to derive pleasure from rape and abuse. Polished people smiling at being used is *not* the extent of sex, even if they appear to be loving people, they don't give you the whole picture, and it's *not your spouse*, so you're letting poison in by viewing something that is meant to be private. <u>You don't need to *learn* or *practice* before your marriage night.</u> The novelty of sex on your wedding night is part of the whole fun of it, even when it isn't as glamorous as in the movies and books.

Two lies we learn growing up:

1. Sex is bad or
2. Sex is worth stealing before marriage.

Sex is very good but people abuse its design. It is worth *preserving* even when we *feel tempted*.

Porn makes us believe sex is wrong, because porn caters to selfish pleasure centers of the brain, and not the sel*fless*, *intimate* knowledge of another person. Porn says that you can have a form of sexual pleasure even while you "are a virgin."

If you start down this path, it will become like a drug: mild at first, but inevitably it will decrease its effects and you'll seek more disgusting, dark, and demeaning versions of the same poison. If you go down that road too far, it can even make you more violent, more apathetic towards true affection and love, and more self-loathing. Good sex in marriage doesn't mean your porn addiction goes away either. There is a heart issue remaining.

Porn is never worth the cost! What you'll risk is too high a cost, but Satan loves to fool people into thinking porn hurts nobody. It doesn't just hurt you; it hurts your future spouse; you'll begin to feel less attracted to them, or start to mistreat them based on what you have seen in these unrealistic scenes.

There are too many distortions of God's original design of sex–bestiality, rape, homosexuality[3]–that are in this world, and you probably see it everywhere, even at school or on YouTube when you're just looking up videos of funny animals or some music video, or in an unwanted advertisement online. Eventually, simply viewing porn isn't enough anymore for some people; now they feel they have to try it, regardless of what their spouse wants. It's a slippery slope, and if you start it, it always gets worse. So don't even start it. It's so difficult to stop. Having a healthy sex life in marriage doesn't protect you from the temptations of sexual sin, but it helps to focus on your spouse. God is the true Healer.

It starts and ends with the heart.

---

[3] I know that at least a quarter or more of my readers will be offended by me saying homosexuality is a distortion of sex. I know, also, that politically and socially, people (including Christians) have failed at loving homosexual people in truth. Love and truth have to go together. Love without truth is "tolerance" of sin. Truth without love is simply ineffective. Perhaps you don't believe it is a sin. That's where we can agree to disagree. I know, though, that just by human anatomy man was meant for woman. Science has made great strides to change bodily appearances, and hearts can easily change by many influences, but I know that the heart of homosexuality is against God's original design. Sex and sexuality aren't just physical; it's first and foremost a heart issue.

Messiah, purity is a word people can't always define, understand, or agree with. We have this resistance from our flesh to be willing to do what the spirit wants, but I pray that we let You guide us to intimacy with You. It is what will guide us to purity in our intimacy with our spouse—them alone, in marriage alone. Purity isn't just bodily; our heart and mind drive what pours out of us, what actions we commit, and what words we say. Let all of our being pursue wholeness, holiness, and righteousness—not for the sake of salvation, but for security in our marriages.

Amen/so be it.

4 ❀ "The One"

*Love for a person requires invested time, patience, and forgiveness,
even when unmerited. It allows for conflict and resolution to shape
two parties into one. It invites an excitement, daily renewed, of
getting to know someone you'll never fully understand, but can't
help trying to. It needs open hands, a guarded heart, and a strong
mind. This love functions correctly only when both parties thrive
on selflessness. It is almost never easy, but it is always worth it.*

IF WE HAD A fairytale marriage, let's be honest, our life would be all
about our spouse, and probably nothing to do with God. Our spouse,
in reality, will at times be too sick, too busy, too angry, and maybe too
unwilling to love you as much as yesterday, and those are the times we tend
to draw nearer to God—hopefully. And if we're honest again, fairytales
(what they have become, not what they originally were) can be predictable,
sometimes boring, and a little unfulfilling. I don't want my marriage to be
like that. I want it to be challenging and rewarding, and trust me, you get
both challenges and rewards when you ask God to lead it.

In a way, marriage the way God designed it can be like a fairytale—one
that is way more full of depth than the ones we read to our children. That
kind of marriage will involve undying commitment to support and love
each other *even when* our spouse does something hurtful, maybe seemingly
unforgiving, and *even when* we experience an extreme loss together.

Now that we understand we won't live a true fairy tale, understand that
also means there isn't a perfect man or Prince Charming. Women, our list
of husband qualities can only go so far. Without a doubt, you need to have
unwavering deal breakers—like they have to love the Lord and you both
need to be on the same page about having a family. First Corinthians 7:39

says "A wife is bound as long as her husband is living. But if her husband dies, she is free to be married to anyone she wants—only in the Lord." If this applies in remarriage, I know it applies in first marriages.

But, ladies, if your husband has a different eye color, or doesn't cook as well as you thought your perfect husband would, or he squeezes the toothpaste the wrong way, he could still be marriage material. In fact, the only thing I think makes a man marriage material is for him to share my values—with God being my Lord, to treat people as God commanded us, to setting boundaries when it comes to time with opposite sex friends, future family desires, and more. Just about everything else—his interests, his general demeanor, the way he problem-solves, how he manages money, and so on— can be different than me.

Sometimes, looking for a potential spouse means we look for similar interests, but what I have found is that opposites attract a lot more than being very alike does. Make sure you share the same values, but what I love so much about my husband is how different we are in basically every other way. From things as small as how "hot" he likes his food (which for him is still basically half frozen), to the fact that he is the pickiest eater in the world and I am the biggest foodie, to things as large as how we handle problems differently[4] and how he is the introvert and I am the extrovert[5]. Also, his hobbies I know so little about, except what I've picked up being married to him. I love it, though, because I learn so much about those interests and can converse with him about it. I sometimes can even participate!

If you're like me, the thought of remarrying if my husband dies before me actually hurts me. My heart is so heavy with the thought. But that's because my husband is alive and well, and I love him so incredibly and am definitely his wife (I checked!). I cannot really imagine having to remarry,

---

[4] Preston is more of the knight in shining armor slaying a dragon; I'm the dragon that blows fire onto my problems to get rid of them quickly, out of my emotion, and I end up burning up some of the good things too by mistake.

[5] Preston's idea of a good time is scrolling Facebook for an hour, Netflixing for a couple hours, and sleeping, and hanging out with friends better be in a fairly private setting because big weddings and whatnot are not where he recharges; as for me, I need human contact about every half hour; the more people, the better, even strangers, because I have no fear walking up and greeting people I don't know; Facebook and Netflix are nice, before I go out and spend time with people for hours at a time!

but this is another serious discussion you should have with your spouse. Scripture is very clear that people do not have to marry or remarry, but they can, (of course within biblical parameters: 1 Corinthians 7:15, Matthew 19:9). The only thing that matters is whether married or not, the Lord needs to remain, well, your Lord. God really is "The One" you need to pursue.

Yahweh, You are the only true God. You are the epitome of oneness, but our understanding of that kind of oneness might lead us to believe only one person can satisfy us. Nobody can 100% of the time except for You. Help us to marry fully to our spouse—their differences that were meant to complement with us, their flaws that were meant to humble us as their spouse, and their willingness to marry us fully right back.

Amen/so be it.

5 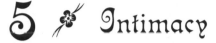 Intimacy

*By choice, not power alone, God is near us—intimately close
enough that we can experience Him, but distant enough
that we don't feel violated or forced into anything.*

Intimacy is not sex. Let's just be clear. Intimacy can involve it, but only, of course, within the marital parameters God has designed it for (because really, isn't it more complicated otherwise?).

With God

How can I be intimate with someone I can't touch or even see with my own eyes? Well, that's a good question. That's the question that could make Christians cold to God or could confuse non-Christians. But you know, sometimes our most intimate experiences in life on earth can be those with God. And I know this is going to sound really "Christianese" but to be intimate with God, you need to pray and spend time in the Bible. This is simple but hard. If you're like me, some days consist of a few minutes in the Bible, and praying can even feel mundane, routine, and ineffective.

Think about your spouse, or your children, or anyone you are close to. How much time do you want to spend with them? It is probably an exorbitant amount (for me I'd want to be with my husband 24/7...some weeks anyway!). Now, how much time do you actually get? Chances are, you make a priority to spend every minute you can with those closest to you, and no matter how busy you are, you make that choice to spend quality time with them. I am confident that if you are around the right people, the more time you spend with them, in true quality time, the more intimate your conversations get, the deeper your connection feels, and the stronger your love for them is, and theirs for you.

The kind of dedication and time you choose for your loved ones should be given to God as well. No, you are not too busy. Satan wants you to think so, and that is one of the biggest lies that humans believe. Another one is that the Bible is confusing. Just take your questions to Godly people or even to reliable online sources and you can find answers. Another hurdle to intimacy with God is the insecurity that we don't "pray well." Yes, there are different types of prayer, but when it comes down to it you just need to talk to God. Usually simpler is better. Our prayers can be silent or spoken aloud, elaborate and full of scripture or a few words from a mournful heart, and can be at any place, anytime.

Let's be honest again, do you even pray over your meals anymore? I know I have passed through many meals without thanking God for it. If my husband made me a meal, he would likely notice and feel hurt if I didn't thank him, even if he didn't ask for a "thank you." (But let's be real, I cook most of our meals anyway!). If you forget to pray for your meals, it doesn't necessarily make you less holy. I am simply pointing out how little a priority prayer seems to be even for Christians. It's used as a last resort, not as the first-call and intimate discussion it is supposed to be.

With Your Spouse

Again, intimacy isn't just sex, but it does involve it. If you chose to read this book, you likely are either married, or will be, so sex will come up. Embrace any section of this book on sex with maturity and an open mind. Some of you may be someone, Christian or not, who feels uncomfortable talking about sex. It isn't necessarily your fault, because you maybe grew up with parents who could barely even say the word "sex" to you. They probably had parents like that too. I'm not knocking that insecurity. I've asked my husband how we would talk to our future children about sex, and at what age; in this world, even our future children will see or hear too many sexually explicit things, so they may already grow up having preconceptions and questions.

Just like time with God in prayer and biblical scripture creates intimacy, time with your spouse and praying with them creates intimacy. Some weeks, I'm thankful to even be in the same room with my husband because we've been so busy we have been ships in the night. I often vent to him about how this world is not designed for Godly marriages. Life keeps us too busy, too selfish, and too undisciplined to spend enough time with our spouse, especially in that *quality time*[6] we talked about.

But guess what! Unlike my husband's sentiment of "that's life," you have a choice! You may be comfortable with busyness, but simplifying your life by eliminating even <u>one thing</u> can make room for true intimacy with your spouse. Do you have weekly dates? Do you kiss your spouse every night? Hopefully you do. But I was in a long distance relationship with Preston, both before marriage, and in the first year or so of marriage. It hurts to not have physical touch, and to not share space with your honey. That's why I'd advise you not to choose long distance, if you have a choice. If you plan to marry, follow your spouse (again, if you have a choice). Military deployment is one of the only reasons you have no choice.

Busyness is hard to avoid these days. I mean, as I write this, I am on a temporary break from working full time and my husband is starting the night (or "graveyard") shift again, and I am afraid we won't see each other *awake* every day. Imagine if I was also still working full time, like most couples. We don't even have children yet. Only an hour ago he left for his monthly drill training for his Air Force commitment. Life is making this somewhat simple situation very difficult to spend quality time with each other. I saw my husband for about twenty minutes before he hit the road. Twenty minutes?! A girl will go crazy…that's not even enough time to talk about what happened today!

My husband has such a calmness about these things; he will say "I just make the most of every moment I get," while my mind is replaying a series of thoughts that go something like …*first of all, I can't even have a decent discussion of my day in less than an hour, and when he is away I have less control over making sure he eats enough, and hydrates enough, and what if something happens to him when he is away from me? Let's not even talk about the fact that I'd love to Netflix for hours with you but no, you have to be responsible*

---

[6] Quality time: Not just sitting next to someone in silence (but it can be); it's more like putting phones away, turning off the TV, and talking, walking, and anything that locks your eyes and, more importantly, your hearts together. You decide what that means for you two.

and provide for us…and I really love that about you. We'd suffer without that.
I know my brain says this is a good problem, to have a full time job for this
provision, but my heart cries for more time with you…

Sound familiar, ladies? I think all of this in my brain on replay every
couple minutes pretty much, on my worst days anyway. I know I am a
worrier and I sometimes make my husband my god—wanting him to be
my all, provide all my security. That isn't good. I admit it as sin. It truly is
easy to get carried away with a pity party playing the hit "Woe is Me" in
your mind, but it comes down to two questions:

1. Do I trust God to take care of my husband? Of me?
2. Will I make the most of my time with him, as scarce as it can be?

I know that when my husband seems to have it all together, he can seem
emotionless, unaffected. That can make me feel crazy! I sometimes wish he
would overreact like I do because I mistakenly think he'd care more about
the problem, and I'd certainly feel less crazy. I am not sure what it'd be like
if he handled problems like I did, but I can tell you we both would have
gray hair (or no hair) if we were both like me! So count your blessings. Be
thankful. I can worry all day he won't come home from his weekend away,
or dwell on how much time I *could* be spending with him, but if I say I trust
in God, then I will actually have to trust Him…even on the day Preston
has to work late, or doesn't come home at all, God forbid…

But let's get back to sex (and all the men reading this say "Oh yes
please!").

"Sex is like a thermometer in marriage, not a thermostat, in that it
measures the health of your intimacy rather than *sets* it." (**Family Life's Art
of Marriage**).

This world makes it easy to be sexually impure before marriage, and
to defile the marriage bed. Between premarital sex, pornography, and even
adultery being readily accessible and normalized, having a fulfilling sex life
with your spouse alone becomes a battle on its own. Now, add on top of that
being exhausted from raising your children, and working all day, and having
arguments with your spouse, and financial struggles, and maybe a recent
death in the family. Will you be rearing to have some steamy sex? The kind
that *gives* and *serves* and *takes its time?* Probably not. It may at best be the

kind that provides a selfish release and more than likely leaves at least one of you unsatisfied.

Emotional and spiritual intimacy need to be nurtured to have the intimacy the marriage bed was meant to provide. Also consider this: sex isn't about your pleasure. In fact, it isn't solely about your spouse's pleasure either. Yes, sex is for procreation and for pleasure, but it's also in its fullest to be an example of oneness with God! Don't misunderstand; our relationship with God isn't sexual, but our walk with God should be more intimate than even the best sex between spouses. In movies and shows, songs, or your own conversations, you might hear "…it's better than sex!" We all can agree sex is pretty amazing (most of the time), and many things in life are awe-inspiring, but God always, always, always has to be first and best! He always is, whether we acknowledge it or not.

Part of oneness with God is to honor Him in your marital sex life, and that means you can't please each other through sinful or abominable means. Things like watching porn *together* doesn't make it right, even if it brings "pleasure." Things like an "open" sexual relationship with more than just your spouse, or doing anything that makes your spouse uncomfortable or out of *equal* control over the kinds of foreplay you both involve yourselves with, are unhealthy and not part of the original design. It will minimize the kind of love you can actually experience. Relational intimacy—or lack thereof—will affect your sexual intimacy.

This may feel too technical, but it is way too important to avoid addressing. There is a special knowledge about the very biology God gave us. Men, know that your wife may not climax from sex alone. Most women don't. It has nothing to do with how good the sex is that you offer, nor is it indicative of her not enjoying it! Some women are completely satisfied without climaxing. Even still, don't assume anything. If she is not climaxing, it simply could be down to:

+ needing more foreplay
+ Or something in her biological makeup that prevents it—at least with sex alone.
+ Or it might just come down to painful sex, which can be avoided with longer foreplay or using lubricant, especially when the menstrual period is close.

Again, technical, but super important—and remember that intimacy *inside* the bedroom measures the intimacy *outside* the bedroom. You may find that investing more effort into your emotional intimacy will help your wife enjoy sex with you more—and may even help her climax.

Women (and men), sex should not be treated as a punishment *or reward*. Some of you might be thinking, *well, why not as a reward?* To put it simply, he may not have earned sex that day, but maybe he still *wants it*. You also may not exactly be the perfect wife one day, but you will still want that sexual intimacy. It can become exhausting and unenjoyable if you, or your spouse, feel that "sexy time" has to be earned—at least if it's a regular habit. Every now and then it wouldn't hurt to say "you have been so helpful at _ _____ so look forward to some time alone with me." Making love could be what recharges you, fulfills you, and motivates you both to be a little better at being a loving spouse *outside the bedroom* tomorrow!

Sex is a duty, yes, but it should be enjoyed fully by both parties. Men are a little different than us women. Women need to feel loved and see our man making an effort for us to *really want sex*. Men need it always, even if you aren't that likeable, or even if you aren't in shape. The doubts and reasons we use to not have sex aren't typical of men to have. Men aren't robots or animals who will die without sex, but it comes pretty close to a *need*. You should thank God they are such visual creatures because no matter your shape and size, they are more than likely thinking of you naked.

As for one regular *nonsexual* act of intimacy my husband and I share, we at least once a quarter, if not monthly or more, will have a "pit and peak" session: no holds barred, all-ears time to hear **each other's pit** (what we could work on in our relationship or as a couple with other people) and **each other's peak** (what is going well or is making us feel most appreciated). This has been a good way to start discussions with my dear husband, and to see if we are on the same page (or not) about unresolved issues or unrecognized victories worthy of celebrating.

Duty of Submission and of Love

God gives us two main commands for marriage in Ephesians 5 and other scriptures (Colossians 3:18–19, Titus 2:5, and 1 Peter 3:1–7). It's funny though because people get this wrong in so many ways. First of all, the command to the wife, though stated first, is shorter than the command to the husband.

1. The wife is to submit to her husband
2. And her husband is to love her as Christ loves the church.

In general, men prefer being respected over being loved, and women prefer being loved over being respected, but we both need love *and* respect. However, Ephesians 5 is famously descriptive—and taken out of context. You'll see it elaborated shortly.

Before I hear from feminists, sexists, and everyone who has been attacked with this passage to justify some painful experiences, know that this passage is actually quite beautiful, and it has to be read in full. Think of the marriage you have, or if you're engaged think of what you want it to be; if this marriage isn't as committed, sacrificing, and passionate as Christ is for us, then we should be striving for that kind of marriage. One way to lay a foundation for this is by listening to this passage.

I will say two important things, though, because these two things are shockingly uncommon nowadays:

1. This passage in Ephesians 5 is one of the many places God specifies men and women marrying, so the fact that we have more openly homosexual marriages could make this very difficult to put into relevant context.
2. Many families have women who "do everything" and "wear the pants" in the marriage, and you even see men portrayed, at best, as incompetent arm candy in commercials and TV shows. The idea of men being "head of the wife" and household (Ephesians 5:23, 1 Corinthians 11:3) is either unheard of, or is very confusing or misunderstood.

Understand this, though: being head of household does not justify abuse nor does it mean women are not *able* to be a strong leader; in fact, women are very capable, but I think head of household in simplest terms means men take on the *ultimate* responsibility for their family. It isn't about *ability* but is about *accountability and authority*. If their family flourishes and triumphs over trials, the husband boosts their family up in support and esteem. If their family suffers in loss or mistakes, the husband takes the hit in carrying the family. If their family experiences great victory, hopefully he is leading the charge, and praising God as his wife and children follow his leadership. This isn't (or shouldn't be) about who has more control.

Even the first couple on earth had this struggle between leadership and submission. Once Adam and Eve sinned, this was God's response:

> "Then he said to the woman, 'I will sharpen the pain of your pregnancy, and in pain you will give birth. *And you will desire to control your husband, but he will rule over you.*" (Genesis 3:16, NLT, emphasis added).

This is *against* God's original plan for man to be a LOVING head of household, and this is why women TEND TO want to do things for their husband, like they are incapable or aren't doing it correctly. Let me try to explain what it means to be a "suitable" and submissive helper (Genesis 2:18, NIV) and what it means to be the loving head of household by sharing some distinctions between the two important roles.

Submissive Helper. Forgive me ladies, but I think that this section will be longer than the men's section for two reasons:

1. God made the command to husbands in Ephesians 5 longer than the section for wives, so I don't need to beat a dead horse, or take away from God's adequate explanation.
2. I am a woman and a wife and thus am motivated to convince every wife and wife-to-be that we have a lot of power—you know, not a dominating kind but an affecting, strong kind—even in our submission to our husbands.

> "Wives, be subject to your own husbands, as to the Lord. For the husband is the head of the wife, as Christ also is the head of the church, He Himself being the Savior of the body. But as the church is subject to Christ, so also

the wives ought to be to their husbands in everything." (Ephesians 5:22–24, NASB).

I know people get hung up on this passage, or they use it sorely out of context to justify abuse, neglect, power, and so on, but I encourage you to watch a message by Central Christian Church's Senior Pastor Cal Jernigan, titled *Hope in the Home*, because he explains the idea of submission beautifully. He touches on several related passages, and he shares some alarming statistics about abuse and how abuse is not the correct way to view submission. In fact, the best way I have heard submission explained was in this message where Cal Jernigan said, "Submission is *voluntary selflessness.*"

Submission is not forced.

Submission is not demanded.

Submission is an act of love through selflessness.

Submission is for women *and men.*

Back in early 2017, my husband and I learned a lot at a class called The Art of Marriage about every aspect of marriage you can think of. Week three we addressed our roles as the submissive helping wife, and the loving headship from the husband.

When we think of *submission* or *helping,* we sometimes think our husbands won't ever help us back, or that we cannot have opinions or make decisions, but it isn't about who has the *sole* say; it's who has the *final* say; it's a cooperative relationship that involves both people. Let's be honest, wives: do you really *want* the final say over huge decisions if they fail or don't pan out? God charges men with that heavy duty and they as men *want that job.* In the class I mentioned above, I heard that "helping involves . . . a vigorous, robust, feminine [followership] that comes alongside a husband as a partner."

Women want to feel loved by their men, but men more than love want *respect.* "There is no more powerful attitude that a wife can have towards her husband than respect." (The Art of Marriage).

Do you realize that in our submissive, most helpful, state of mind, we can provide a *powerful* and extremely *influential* change in our husbands? Nagging doesn't work. Doing it for them may work, but it really hurts our husbands because "for most men, their deepest fear is failure and their deepest need is the kind of confidence only a wife can provide." (The Art of Marriage).

I must add that if any change occurs in our husbands, it's God working *through us*, not us changing our spouse.

Ladies, we all know our men don't always use maps and sometimes we get lost. I know that they can't do some things like you, but unlike what society and media says, our husbands are capable fathers, loving husbands, and are designed to work hard to provide for your family. They deserve our respect, even when they fail or make mistakes. Yes, even then. How amazed would your husband be if he forgot to do that errand he should have done yesterday and instead of saying "How could you forget again?" you say "Oh that's okay, honey; you have been working so hard for us that it's really no big deal." In any situation you could say "I told you so," *or* you can say "Anybody can make a mistake. What can I do to help you?"

Now women, I'm going to touch a nerve here, but in all our girl talk—and for some of us, the *pure gossip* we should be avoiding anyway—let's make sure we talk with women who will give us sound, Godly counsel. Have friends who will tell you hard truths, offer genuine encouragement, and who will pray with and for you; don't get friends who only say what you want to hear, and who are determined to make you a strong, independent woman within your marriage. While co-dependence can be unhealthy, complementary teamwork is not; while being a strong, capable woman is admired and still okay in our homes and workplaces, humble and yielding wives should also be who we are.

Know that you do not need to submit to abuse or immorality. God is always first in the best marriages, so if your husbands take advantage of you or want you to jeopardize your integrity, you have free will for a reason and you can find help through *or out* of the marriage if necessary.

Head of Household. Unfortunately, many women *want* a sort of control in marriage, and society encourages this; it's not always terrible for women to advise her husband, because you're both a team, but I think men have a divine role appointed by God, and *control* shouldn't be coming from either spouse. That includes men as they lead. Just as forced sex in marriage is still rape, forced obedience is still a control-issue and does not capture the essence of "the head" that Christ laid out in loving the church.

"Husbands, <u>love your wives, just as Christ also loved the church and gave Himself up for her</u>, so that He might sanctify her, having cleansed her by the washing of water with the word, that He might present to Himself the church in all her glory, having no spot or wrinkle or any such thing; but that <u>she would be holy and blameless</u>. So husbands ought also to <u>love their own wives as their own bodies</u>.

He who loves his own wife loves himself; for no one ever hated his own flesh, but nourishes and cherishes it, just as Christ also does the church, because we are members of His body. For this reason a man shall leave his father and mother and shall be joined to his wife, and the two shall become one flesh. This mystery is great; but I am speaking with reference to Christ and the church." (Ephesians 5: 25–32, NASB, emphasis added).

Headship means that the man *sacrifices* himself for the sake of his family. Headship also means that the man has the burden of *taking the initiative* to move things forward on behalf of his family. Doesn't sound like the kind of headship we've seen, heard of, or experienced, huh? Women aren't always "holy and blameless (v. 27)" but the man presents his wife like Christ presents the Church—broken, but holy and blameless through God. Men, you do everything you can to present your wives this way, even when she fails you. Her example should be you, and your example should be God. She and your children look up to you.

"Woman, get me a sandwich" is not true headship. That at best is laziness, and at worst may be a sign of a control issue. True leadership is taking responsibility for the decisions made for *and with* your family, husbands.

Let's dig into this deeper.

Husbands and wives, what makes you feel most loved? If you check out Gary Chapman's *The 5 Love Languages*, you can discover that answer. For me, physical touch and quality time are my top two ways to feel loved. For my husband, physical touch and words of affirmation are his. You may find out that you have very opposite love languages, and that may require a bit more sacrifice on your part, especially if only one of you has physical touch as your top three, and one does not. Physical touch is probably the most *outward* measurement of the intimacy a marriage has, so when one person's love language is physical touch and the other spouse has physical touch as a low priority in feeling loved, it can take more effort to genuinely love this way.

The point is, no matter how you feel loved most, we women really desire feeling cherished and protected more than we would want to feel acknowledged and respected. Of course, we want both, but typically we would rather be held and told "I love you" than we would want to be looked in the eyes with a pat on the shoulder and be told "you did so well today."

Our husbands still need to be told we love them, of course, and shown it in their love language ways, but think about how you can respect your husband. Here are some ideas:

1. **Give him some space** when he gets home from work to get comfortable, unwind, and recharge, and **give him a hot meal** before you unload on him your wonderful achievements—or terrible catastrophes—from the day.
2. **Thank him** for all the chores he does, even when he is exhausted or didn't finish the chores all the way just yet.
3. **Compliment him** in front of his friends, and in private when you're both alone.
4. **Let him drive without the map**, even if you get lost; **trust him** to find the way (this one can be hard for me who uses my mapping app all the time).

These are just a few, but surely you can think of more specific things.

Let's get to the nagging question…how do we *submit* without being walked on? Here's the thing: submission has more to do with the respect we just talked about than it does with how we feel. I am not saying you should stay quiet and give little effort towards your wifely and motherly duties. In fact, we should speak often with our husbands, while we listen even more, and sometimes we should let our husbands make a mistake here and there to show that we don't need to coddle him. Besides, sometimes what we view as a mistake is simply a *different way* of accomplishing the same task. So what if it takes longer, or was done *too* quickly!

If your husband shouts saying "you need to submit because it's in the Bible" as he beats you, yells at you, or neglects you in any way, then he is wrong and you are being mistreated. Remember men, this passage says to love your wife as Christ loves the church, so your responsibility is high. Not only will you take the hits when your family suffers loss or consequences to mistakes, but you should be willing to lay down your life like Christ, to be generous in time, affection, and money, and to teach your family how to follow God, like Jesus did. You have no small task, and this is part of the issue with our societal shift in women being head of household. We teach girls, even in princess-warrior-type movies, that they can be pretty, strong, and independent, and that we don't really need men. We leave nothing for our men to be or do when we say we can do it all on our own. At the same time, men need some tenderness and well-rounded love too. Trust me, my man is at his best when his home is clean and orderly, when his stomach is fed, and when his wife desires him.

Wives, submission is not saying you should never speak your mind, never make choices, and allow your husband to beat you with rods and words. Submission essentially is to yield to your husband's leadership and to support him *through* your gifts, and involves sharing your thoughts and choices with him. The way submission is *supposed* to be is quite opposite of what the world *says* submission should be.

Husbands, you are to love your wives as Christ loves the church. The first part of this is loving her. That does not imply she is not to love you back. We cannot have submission without love. Likewise, husbands, you cannot love your wife if you belittle her and turn submission into control, power, and abuse.

I think deep down we all know this. But if we put the God sticker on our actions, and twist a scripture around it, we tend to believe it. *People complicate scripture and justify wrongdoings, not the LORD.* So let's spend time with the Lord first (in prayer and in scripture) then spend time with our spouse. Similar principles apply to our children. That is the order: First God, then spouse, then children. When we put those 3 out of order, emptiness grows, hurt happens, and sometimes we lose more than we bargained for.

God created man first, but His deciding to create woman also is not to say men are incompetent and inadequate. In fact, it was for man's benefit and supplement that Eve was made. One of my favorite quotes best describes the balance of submission and love:

> Seventeenth century minister and author Matthew Henry said "Eve was not taken out of Adam's head to top him, neither out of his feet to be trampled on by him, but out of his side to be equal with him, under his arm to be protected by him, and near his heart to be loved by him."

Understanding Each Other's Personality

Let's talk about extroversion and introversion. I guarantee you, most of you married or almost-married couples are one extrovert and one introvert.

The Myers Briggs Personality Test is one of the most comprehensive ways to figure this out. If you have taken it before, I invite you to take it again, because it can change over time. Encourage your spouse or child to take it too.

Your personality result is not *just* about extroversion versus introversion. That's just one part. My personality type is ESFJ, The Consul, and each letter stands for Extroversion, Sensing, Feeling, and Judging.

Let me explain simply that INTROVERSION does not necessarily mean the person is SHY, has no friends, and can't socialize well; EXTROVERSION does not necessarily mean the person is loud, talkative, pushy, and lives life for the sole purpose of small talk.

Being extroverted or introverted is innate. Natural. And it is not necessarily indicative of a person's habits. For example, an extroverted person, *who gets recharged by being around people,* may be stuck in a job with long hours and thus sleeps inside their house a lot, and may be presumed an introvert because people don't see them outside their home much. But they could get *recharged* by being around people which they often cannot do.

On the same token, an introvert may socialize well, but may be *getting exhausted* by it. It comes down to what recharges you. My friend Bob once said that he is introverted (which I was surprised by when he told me) but he is a "professional extrovert." I didn't understand the terms well when he told me; I was in high school. All I knew was, at best, that an introvert like him can't be this successful at talking with so many people; that is utterly not true—at least in most cases.

Let's break this down some more.

When I talk—often a lot and at length—that is how I process information, and it sometimes takes a while to get to my point, but I don't even always know what my point is until I have reached it by talking aloud. This might be partly why, in pre-marital counseling years ago, I learned I wasn't as attentive a listener as I thought. My husband, in comparison, was better at that. While I, the extrovert, was the one who could better articulate what I wanted and what I felt, he as the introvert was not. His strength was *listening*, and mine was *talking*. Again, it's just true for us and not every couple.

Introverts reading this are probably thinking about how different they are from me; usually they think and process BEFORE they speak—if at all.

About my assertive talking, though—it isn't a bad thing! I mean, I have a problem *interrupting* people—ever since childhood—and I can ramble. I tend to communicate what I *want* and *feel* a lot better than my husband; he is better at *attentive listening* surely because he is an introvert. To communicate well, you need to practice both.

When I talk a lot, I am not trying to be rude. I just have so much to say. My talking to you so much is how I show you I value your company and opinion, and want to discuss matters. And no, not just the weather. In fact, I don't care for small talk; it tends to be insincere, like 'the weather's nice,' and 'yeah, I'm fine.'

Awkward silence is still awkward for me, but I don't find an excuse to walk away; I ask another question, or I tell them something I like about them, or I invite them to walk with me to a new area. It either ends the conversation, or ends the awkwardness. Extroverts have a higher tolerance for *awkward* silence because they can quickly talk about something else to *replace that dead air*, but they can't *stay* in silence like introverts can when it's just hanging out. Extroverts want to *fill* the silence, while introverts want to *leave* the awkward silence—unless it's with other introverts. It's a very strange thing.

As an extrovert, I forfeit *being with others* as often as I'd like (basically every few hours daily) so I can stay inside with my introverted husband, which I actually love too. As an introvert, I am sure he forfeits *comfort* and *energy* by talking with people when we are *out*. Even talking with *me* exhausts him, I'm sure. In marriage, compromise happens daily.

I don't know as much about introversion except what I know about my husband, a few introverted friends, and the fact that all my siblings and parents are introverted. Literally, I inherited the extroversion from maybe a great grandparent or something.

Back to this dynamic in marriage. My husband, when coming home from a long day at work, would rather listen to his HAM (Hertz-Armstrong-Marconi) radios than discuss something with me right away. This is especially the case if it has to do with what's on our to-do list, money that I want to spend, or anything philosophical or requires extreme focus. When he is at home unwinding, he prefers to scroll Facebook in quiet than perhaps to talk to me about my day—at least if the goal is to relax.

He will talk to me when he has unwound his mind, of course. It helps if he has eaten too! Good thing I am a decent cook.

He would rather listen to his scanners and program his radios than be in a large group of friends discussing something, even something lighthearted, though he values friendship deeply.

At weddings and events, he would rather snack on the side and people-watch. Me? I'm the one greeting strangers and probably connecting with them on social media by the end of the day.

A misconception about EXTROVERTS is that all extroverts like small talk. But me, I am not in that boat. We are good at it and tolerate it, but I wanna get to the juice. You tell me you're fine? I'm not only going to ask you *why* you're fine, but I'm most likely gonna find out you're actually *not* fine.

I've hugged a stranger who is now my friend.

I have sung in front of strangers.

I am the one hugging friends in church when the pastor says to shake hands, and my husband shakes one person's hand silently and then sits down. He's not being rude; he is just less comfortable with forced interaction.

I get truly depressed when I don't have human interaction every single day, multiple times a day.

Both personality traits are natural and useful and both need to bend when in a marriage.

I find that there is a lot more content, research, and sensitivity towards those who are introverted, and I am sure it partly has to do with how misunderstood they are. In fact, both personality types are a relatively new study. It's important to know, so share it with your spouse, your kids, and whoever else could benefit from knowing how you operate *naturally*. It's also important so your extroverted friends don't get offended when you introverts let their call go to voicemail about setting a date to hang out, and so your introverted friends can feel appreciated when you extroverts invite them over to talk about life—again!

In marriage, figure out how you both recharge, along with how you both manage money, how you discipline, and so on. If you don't know *how* to discover it, you soon will! Sometimes, it just takes asking your spouse what they prefer in every situation, and if it differs from you, figure out a compromise, or take turns (i.e. one week go *out* on a double date, and another week, stay *in* and binge watch Netflix by yourselves without talking).

My God, somehow intimacy has turned into a dirty word. Intimacy is not about sex alone. In fact, intimacy starts with the heart. I pray that we desire to be intimate in the most vulnerable ways, appropriately with You and with our (future) spouse. Whatever we are afraid will reveal itself as we open up with You as God and with our marital partner. I pray intimacy will become the bridge between indifferent marriages and fulfilling ones.

Amen/so be it.

6 ✿ The Honeymoon

Relationships of any kind, but especially of the romantic kind, do not take, but receive thankfully and give unconditionally. There are beautiful things that we must wait for in these relationships, but those beauties are never the only aspect to a relationship—even a marriage.

I WILL BE THE FIRST to tell you that my first week married, as mentioned earlier, in this beautiful Flagstaff cabin in Arizona, was *literally* a physically painful journey. It took a very long time, even after the honeymoon week, to feel like the *actual* "first time." Let me tell you, movies don't ever make it look realistic. Now as you continue to read this chapter, I'd continue to read it through the lens of a mature adult. The church doesn't talk about sex that much, and when some do, it is sometimes in the wrong way. This is just an honest discussion.

It is not common to hear about a man, who had been with a couple women before, withhold sexual intimacy from you until marriage out of respect for you. Trust me, we both *wanted* that sexual intimacy, but we wanted *more* to experience it at the right time. It took a strong man, my husband, to wait until marriage as if he was brand new, still a virgin. He was, and is, a man after <u>God's</u> heart, not his own heart, and not mine alone either.

You might be reading this thinking...*okay, but seriously, a man being a virgin nowadays isn't that appreciated. And I want my man experienced...it doesn't bother me if he isn't a virgin.* But you know, I think marriage, at least that first night, is supposed to be a new learning experience: confusing, messy, and challenging. It is the reward for waiting; it is the finish line and the starting line all at once, and the proclamation to your spouse that you would wait longer if you had to, despite how torturous it was, because they are worth it.

Did the painful and seemingly endless trial and error I experienced make it not worth it? NOT IN THE LEAST. I still enjoyed my husband *because* we had waited. It wasn't just tab A into slot B either. I'm sorry for the meager and tasteless analogy, but some people seem to treat sex this way, treat *people* this way. We had a guilt-free week of sexual intimacy to match our emotional intimacy we married into. We didn't have to have this movie-perfect love scene to feel loved and to gain God-designed pleasure from each other. Did you see that? God designed us for this (among other things). It is not a sin to desire someone this way. He just warns us of lustful thoughts and of sexual sin. It's in the *discipline* we experience the *divine*.

Not long after some well-deserved practice *with each other*, sexual interactions with my husband have become beautiful and we can comfortably learn about each other without the pain I endured for the longest month of my life.

The joy of waiting, if you're both pure, is that you have nothing in your life experiences to compare it to.

The joy of waiting, if only *one* of you is pure, or if both of you are not, is that you have time in the engagement to become new, to learn what it is like to abstain from something meant for marriage. I know it is a fight, but that's part of what makes it so sacred. My own husband and I were engaged a year and a half (a half a year longer than planned), which likely made my husband's thought life for our married night that much freer, and his desire for me that much stronger. It almost was as if he really was new for me. But know this, it was a fight for him daily. I know this from discussions with him.

Now if you are not yet married, please hear me. I know you're in one of these three groups:

1. Both of you are virgins
2. Only one of you is a virgin
3. Both of you are *not* virgins

All groups of people have a choice: continue in sin, or don't.

At some point, you decide…is my future spouse worth waiting for? I understand if you've already broken this, you think you can't start over. Physically, you have experience, and mentally you have memories, but you can still decide to commit to this challenge, or not to.

Also, pray with each other to endure. Don't snuggle in their bed naked, alone with them, and hope you don't do anything. You'll either struggle with your thought life as your flesh and spirit fight against each other, or you'll give in and fall. Your dates should be in public and, as often as you can, with strong men and women of God. Any way you'll be around people who will keep you accountable but still give you time to enjoy your loved one's company is the way to go. Think back to the two scenarios from earlier, and how scenario two gave two people that opportunity for attractive glances even while out with friends.

You both may decide to have discussions about what you expect night one, and what lines not to cross, perhaps. I'm confident I don't have to be detailed about that one. That is between you two as mature, God-fearing adults.

Women, I am mostly talking to you about this one: it may not feel that good at first. Men, be patient. Being with your spouse sexually is best when you are emotionally intimate; entering marriage should be on that foundation as it is. Then, when it comes down to physical intimacy, take it as a gift and savor it. God gave us hands and lips, not just ...well, you know, other parts. It isn't a quick transaction. It is an experience to be treasured, and multiple times. You decide how frequent. And the chapter of difficulty that you both pass through will be nothing compared to the other side. It's also possible it won't be painful for the woman.

Just remember to be on the same page with your (future) spouse about waiting until marriage.

A few practical tips for the honeymoon:

1. **Are you going to make a road trip that same day, exhausted after the wedding, or will you wait a day or so to make that trip?** Once you're deemed married, you don't have to wait for sex, but you may decide to delay the *trip itself* after a night's sleep. My husband and I left the same day, ready to escape to our beautiful Flagstaff cabin. Plus, we didn't have our own place yet, so it was the most practical choice, and the reservation was in place.

2. **Make sure you plan time <u>outside the bedroom</u> too**. Make it a full first trip as husband and wife. I mean, unless you're both introverts!

3. **Take your wedding cards** and gather all the money inside to take to spend for the honeymoon (and maybe save some too, because newlyweds can actually be financially smart too).

4. Don't spend too much time opening gifts before the honeymoon; save it for after, so you can **come home to another celebration.**

5. **Ladies, pick out something nice to wear for your husband.**

6. **If you don't want a positive pregnancy test a month after getting married, make sure you come prepared.** My husband and I wanted a few years married, just us, before actively trying for children, and since we didn't want to abstain from sex within our marriage for years, obviously, we needed to take precautions. It doesn't always take less than a month to conceive, but it can!

Precautions can be the pull-out method, but it isn't fool-proof. Also, condoms are fine, and if you as the wife are okay with the side effects birth control can have, then to each his (or her) own. I didn't want to pop pills or experience negative symptoms, or to have something else to remember every day.

Again, discuss it and agree with each other in prayer about these things.

Creator, we acknowledge that You created sex. I pray that the time spent immediately upon becoming married will include sex that is as painless and as satisfying as You designed it. I pray that space is left to be a couple outside the bedroom too, if it is desired. Use every couple reading this to see marriage differently, to see sex differently, than the world does. Honeymoons don't have to be expensive to be intimate, and marriages don't have to be free of mess to be beautiful. Use this time of newness as a married couple to heal wounds if either spouse wasn't a virgin upon marrying each other. This can be a starting point, not an ending.

Amen/so be it.

7 ❧ Prayer

Prayer is not necessarily about telling God what is on your heart, not only. He already knows. Prayer is for you too—to change you and to prepare you.

BEFORE I TALK ABOUT actual prayer, I want to talk about talking and communicating *with each other*. As I write this, I am at an Air Force base for my husband's Air Force reserves commitment. A couple of hours ago, my husband came back to our temporary home[7] to have lunch with me because on these weekends, I usually stay in. At the end of this hour with him, I decided to start a conversation by asking "What is your most favorite and least favorite quality about me?"

Now let's pause. Men and women react differently to this question. Women genuinely want an honest answer to this question, but we aren't always emotionally prepared for that second part of the question. Men try not to answer the second question, even when asked, and they skirt around it with a generic answer. For those men (and women) who do answer that difficult question, they tend to think of something that *isn't* really their *least* favorite quality, or they think of something that *is* their least favorite quality, but they make it sound like a strength. It's like when asked during interviews what your weakness is and you make it sound like a strength: "I tend to dwell so much on the negative things that it helps me problem-solve."

---

[7] It seems as though every time we go to this base, we have a different experience with the living situation. Last time we were here, I was stuck in an all-male dorm of sorts and asked my husband to just drive me back home 2 hours away, the next morning. This time, we basically got our own fully stocked apartment that would have been almost as nice as our honeymoon spot! You never know what you'll get on these drill weekends!

When I asked this question, I wasn't surprised by my husband's answer to the first part. He essentially said I have an open and loving heart that serves him well. For the second part, I expected he would address my being too busy or too worrisome. But my sweet husband in his wisdom, trying to be as honest as he could, warned me he didn't want to share his answer because it may hurt me. I urged him a couple times to tell me anyway, and he said "I think you could lose some weight in your belly."

All you women reading may be torn between the bravery in his candid honesty and the aftermath of bringing up a sore spot for many females, and you may be thinking *how dare he say such a thing...*

Please understand that this—exercise, our self dislikes, what we eat, etc.— is something we often discuss. It's not like I was surprised that I'm not as in-shape as I should be. But there was a misunderstanding; I expected him to read my mind and only answer to my *personality* and not bring up the one thing I hate most about my body. (Literally five times in my life people thought I was pregnant, but I never have been!). Being the realistic and genuine husband he is, Preston thought I was asking about one thing (physical or not) that needed improvement. Imagine how I felt when I basically heard him say my belly is his *least favorite* quality about me. Now all I want to do is get rid of it because I'm obviously not sexy to him anymore, right?

Wrong.

In consequence, we calmly explained what we were feeling, exchanged a couple of hugs, and I vowed to him and myself that I was going to exercise regularly again, and I want to exercise *with him*; it motivates me to have him as a rallying friend exercising too. He even bought an exercise ball for me that I wanted. Through financial investment in my decision, he was showing his full support to me, not saying I was too fat for him.

But onto the point: If communicating to a human can be this shaky, imagine what talking to an invisible God is. Even still, keep in mind communicating with Him is *simple!* Talk regularly, and talk honestly. Bring your requests to God and praise Him like a child would—often and with all emotion attached. You don't *need* to quote scripture when you pray, but you can. Don't complicate things. Just lay out all your sin, baggage, emotions, and heartache. You don't have to fake smile with God.

Praying With Your Spouse

Let me just say that praying with my husband is so relieving. Usually, I get to hear my husband in his most honest, unfiltered thoughts. And we hold hands to make it a special experience. Sometimes we even hug while we pray. You can pray with your spouse at night before you sleep, in the morning when you wake, on the drive to work when you pass a car wreck, before meals in and out of the house, and anytime else. Pray because you want to pray with them, not because you want people to think you look super spiritual, because Pharisees prayed publicly and loudly so they looked good and were seen by people (Matthew 6:5), but their hearts weren't that transformed.

I'd also advise you not to bring up something really heavy or about your spouse right in the middle of prayer—not if it's the first time they hear about it anyway. If you both close your eyes and hold hands to pray one night and you share *God, I pray that you help my husband to not stare at my best friend's cleavage when she comes to visit,* imagine his reaction when he realizes you've noticed, you're hurt, and now he is embarrassed and may not be focused on prayer but on how to keep his eyes closed around every female. There are serious burdens we bring to the Lord, and He can handle them, but we are still human and need to be sensitive to our spouse. Bring up issues *on your own* to God, then discuss it with your spouse, and if necessary pray about it more *with your spouse, or on your own some more.*

I would suggest praying *with* your spouse *about* others. It is powerful to pray as a couple for friends and family—especially the ones that drive you crazy! And ask your spouse what they need prayer for personally too. You don't always have to hope you pray the right thing. Just pray directly and specifically over something your spouse needs prayer for. Being married, it might involve you too.

Praying For Your Spouse

If you are not yet married, you can still pray for your spouse! You may be engaged, or maybe you haven't met them yet, but finding a spouse (especially for women who want to be pursued by a special man) should not be taken lightly. I am not saying you need to have a list of 100 attributes your husband should have—such as cooking your 3 favorite meals every week and that he should have blue eyes. I *am* saying you *shouldn't settle* just because he is good looking, or for really any superficial quality. First of all, <u>he needs to love the Lord</u>. He shouldn't just go to church or serve the church—there is a difference between just going to church and actually loving Jesus. His life should be transformed, he needs to respect purity (even if he isn't a virgin), and he should look very different spiritually from the world. And yes, he can have blue eyes, be good looking, and cook! Just don't make those deal-breakers, okay?

Another difficult thing…*what if he doesn't pray for me?* You know what, your spouse may *not* be praying for you regularly, or at all. But marriage involves a lot of sacrifice, and praying for someone who may not pray for *you* is always hard. A reality, though, is that a lot of what we bring to God can improve by praying about it, especially when it is a prayer to change *ourselves first*.

If you are not sure what to pray about, here are some suggestions (husbands, you can modify these for your wife):

1. That he would be surrounded by Godly men, who would not stir him into temptations.
2. That he would pray and spend time in God's Word with you, and on his own.
3. That he would know his worth, even when income is low and mistakes are high.
4. That he would love his children tenderly, but strongly too.
5. That he would pray for his children and spend quality time with them.
6. That he would make quality time with you a priority, even before the kids.
7. That he would do his work well, and never jeopardize his integrity.
8. That he is protected as he drives and works and defends his family in any circumstance.

For Myself

I am sure a lot of married people bring requests of depression, pain from infidelity, struggles with a loss, and other huge afflictions to God, but asking God to give *you* peace or to give *you* wisdom is just as powerful as asking God to help your husband with his porn addiction (or the wife with hers), for example. Always think and pray about how God can work on *you* as God works on your spouse.

Stormie Omartian wrote one of my favorite books, *The Power of a Praying Wife*. It isn't my favorite because it was easy to cover certain topics. Some of it was difficult, like the idea of praying for a spouse who may or may not be praying for you. It is my favorite because it has made me 180 degrees more intentional in how I pray for, and speak to, my husband.

Remember: keep prayer regular and honest. It can be short and consist of sobs with the name *Jesus* whispered in an empty bed at night; it can be intimate and lengthy as you hold your spouse's hand in the middle of your unborn child's nursery; it can be done with your children in your living room every day as they sit on your lap, still learning to talk; it can be done on the road (with eyes open) as you pass by that accident or strip club. . . Just remember: pray.

Emmanuel, we pray to you honestly and authentically. We think falsely that we have to use theological words or scripture to be heard, so we stop talking to You altogether. We confess that as sin. We fall short of You always. But we need You, so we thank You for opening a way for us to talk to You and to listen long afterward. Challenge us to pray for others more than ourselves, and to listen after we talk. Show us where prayer create change and spur growth in our marriage. I pray that we pray before we act, speak, or even think too long on anything, even the good things.

Amen/so be it.

8 ❀ What About Me?

Give everything, your WHOLE life and love, because at least you know you would've never held back for the cause of the Kingdom; expect NOTHING in return, because at least you can <u>accept</u> when nothing is returned, and you'll be overjoyed when anyone does give back.

I THINK WHERE THE WORLD has gotten marriage wrong the most is seeking marriage for what *I* can get from *the one*, as opposed to seeking marriage for what you can *give* to *the one* and how you can mimic the model of Christ and the church through marriage. If you aren't Christian, truly living for the Lord, your marriage may not have that goal of being like God and the church (Revelation 22:17), but mine is. I am sure it is the richest form of marriage, and is the most rewarding goal—even though we never reach Godly *perfection*.

In this world, we face many things when we choose to be that close to another human being. The most basic thing we face as a married couple is offering quality time in this busy way of life, between work, friends, children, errands and chores, and being plain tired. But choices have to be made, sometimes truly sacrificially, to balance it all.

You and your spouse need to have rules for your marriage, even beyond what you vowed to friends and family at the wedding. My husband and I have decided on a few core things:

1. Never even *threaten* divorce, no matter how angry.
2. We are not to be with an opposite sex friend without either each other or another trustworthy person present (hopefully of the same sex as ourselves).

3. Never end the night without resolving an issue that has upset us; at least, we have to *discuss* it and not go to bed angry, and *resolve* it in the morning.

We certainly come across other guidelines along the way, and I know some couples do not abide by *our* rules, but we know why we have them and you will need to address your own rules. Issues regarding money languages (see *Managing God's Money* by Randy Alcorn) and ways we feel most loved (see "Love Languages" resource) are the biggest ways to get to know your spouse and how to avoid a lot of big fights.

Now let's talk about fights, arguments, disagreements, whatever you call them...they will happen. I think we all know that by now, but we need to fight the right way. Being an attentive listener is one of the first things. Being attentive while listening means that you aren't thinking about what you'll say in response to what your spouse has—or has not—said, not until *after* they finish speaking. Also, make sure that you look your spouse in the eyes when he/she speaks. But when it's your turn to speak, make sure it's still honoring. Use "I feel" more than "You did" phrases. The goal is to listen to understand, not to listen to respond.

Think of it this way: If you both are heated about something with each other, and you say something extremely hurtful (or even if you choose the right words and use the wrong *tone of voice*), maybe your spouse is upset enough that he takes a drive[8]. While driving upset, he doesn't pay attention to that truck about to hit him, and he dies. Would you want your *last conversation* to be *the last one he heard?*

I know it's a painful example, but I often think about this, and unfortunately it's usually after I speak to my husband in a dishonorable way. I don't know how many times I've heard of people regretting their most recent conversation with someone right before they die. The truth is, we don't know when we will leave this planet so, as much as possible, treat your spouse like you did in your honeymoon phase, but with the mentality of an

---

[8] If you or your spouse need to take a drive to cool off, that's okay, but maybe communicate where you plan to go and when you plan to come back. That way, your spouse knows where to find you and when to worry or come looking for you, if something were to happen.

experienced marriage, like God treats us, the church. Always ask yourself if that most recent conversation you had with your spouse would satisfy them if they died today. (And of course, don't live in fear that they will die today, or tragically. It'll wreck you, trust me).

Sometimes love is telling your spouse how proud you are of their work, even though they worked a lot longer than you wanted and all you want to do is snuggle for hours watching Netflix and unload about your day.

Sometimes love is hiding your tears and crying without your spouse knowing (ladies!) so he doesn't falsely feel like a failure; even when you're sad for other reasons, men sometimes carry a burden thinking they caused pain. They feel helpless when they can't zap it away.

Most of the time, though, love is being able to *openly cry* with each other, and praying for each other, being a teammate and friend—a best friend.

When my husband and I went to Wichita Falls in Texas on temporary duty for a retraining, we had JUST bought a new house in Arizona. In Texas, we got put in what was similar to the one bedroom apartment we just moved out of, only it was the on-base Inn, and this extroverted girl (that's me) had some adjusting to do. We didn't have an oven, and we had a tiny fridge. Even the convection oven we bought to make do made me feel so... unwifely. I was used to making elaborate meals that took time... Thankfully, our friends bought us a Hot Plate, which was the next best thing to that missing oven. And don't get me started about the (lack of) counter space…

We left our second vehicle, my vehicle, back in Arizona because it wasn't fit for travel, nor could his vehicle safely haul it with us. So here I am, trapped in a small temporary home, ready to burst when my husband walks through the door from work because my only transportation was my own two feet, and nothing is even close enough to walk to except the ice machine, the Commissary, and the laundry room. To top it off, we share a quick meal for ten minutes, and after not seeing him all day, he gets to studying for hours.

He had to. Every day he was "fire-hosed" with content and wanted to succeed the FIRST time, or they will fail, which his instructors "scare tacticted" them, as Preston put it, into believing from day one. I was actually proud to see him take this so seriously. He has always worked hard for us, but I'm selfish and missed him and wanted him all to myself. And yes, I cried a little on my own. I wrote in my journal complaining to God a little. I told my husband with a smile that he is going to do so well, and I asked him if he needed anything, keeping back my selfish frustration.

Sometimes love is completely about what you give, and you give beyond even that.

In disagreements, if your spouse says "I can't do this right now," then I'd urge you to listen and respect that wish. Otherwise, what you have to say may fall on deaf ears. Even if you're right! One of you needs more time to process a problem or needs to decompress from the day before addressing an issue.

Your spouse may be too tired or too upset to respectfully and lovingly resolve the issue. You don't have to wait a week. I'd advise against it, in fact. But waiting an hour or two can help make problem resolution much more effective.

I was discouraged one day that my husband had his phone out during one of my choir concerts. At one point, he even had his laptop out because we just hours prior got back from camping and he had work to do. Granted, he had seen me sing these songs at least 5 times the past few months and he probably would have fallen asleep to our angelic voices if it weren't for his phone. Also, it would have been worse if he sat in front, but I felt it was rude nonetheless. I'm shocked none of the conservative senior citizens next to him reprimanded him for his *millennial*-like stereotype of electronic use.

Eventually, at one point in the concert, we glanced at each other and by my face he could tell I was saying *"Put that computer away!"* and he did. Spouses know each other like that. But I was still sure to let him know in the car afterward that I appreciated him putting the computer away because it was rude to have it out; however, I respected him when he said "I can't do this right now," even though I wanted to discuss how I believe he could have worked on his computer in a different room or something. I wanted him to apologize *right then* in the car and validate me, but my exhausted husband couldn't deal with talking it through yet. What I wanted to say could wait. Next, I could use the undesired twenty minutes of silence to think *calmly* on the rest of the way home about what I'd say and how I could say it—respectfully, of course. It's nice to argue with your spouse *in your head*, then to calmly discuss something *out loud*—blowing off steam *before* your attack a problem.

Part of loving my husband and learning about him comes from how he and I are so different in how we handle problems, and we complement each other. However, it can also put pressure on each other (even if handling problems identically were to have its own issues).

My husband encounters a problem then goes into hibernation on the matter until it falls through naturally, or if the problem has reared its ugly head tenfold. But me...I think about everything that will mess up in our life because of a problem that hasn't happened yet, and I go trying to fix it—all of it, all at once. Sometimes before there is even a problem. Since almost always it has to do with our schedule, and I maintain our schedule, I start going into overdrive.

September of 2016 marked a very transitional point in our lives because of Preston's work schedule. You see, he went from one bad work schedule to another; he was working overnights Sunday through Thursday, which tore up his sleep schedule and rendered our time together during the day almost non-existent.

Then, he was told that come early to mid-October, he would be working days but that included weekends. I started digesting the fact that we wouldn't sit at church together or even *serve* at church together anymore. I'd have to drive alone. And forget about him coming to my monthly Sunday evening choir concerts. He would have to suffice with church online; some churches don't even have that much.

Then I thought about an already-paid-for men's event in Northern Arizona on October 22nd, and a friend's wedding the next weekend that he was assigned to walk the bride down in. Would we get our money back for the men's retreat, which (by the way) we purchased the first day it was announced? An event he missed the year prior too! Would his employer let him go to these events in exchange for a different day in the week? Will he still be able to walk our friend down the aisle, let alone arrive on time? In the end, these are relatively small problems in life, you know, first world problems. But I kid you not, I start bawling at the idea of anything being out of its place. I am a *worrier*. My husband's more of a *warrior*.

These are things my husband likely already knew about these events upon being told about his shift change, but I lack grace when I'm in mission mode, and I made a difficult change even harder on him. I make his problem-solving process, or lack thereof, almost impossible.

I had always trained myself to not reward myself until a task is finished.

I wouldn't eat dinner until I finished homework. I don't watch TV until I get chores done. And I certainly don't rest in the assurance that I won't have to sleep alone anymore until we've figured out how all our weekend commitments can resolve themselves. I can be pretty pessimistic.

In marriage, you realize a lot about yourself through how you both deal with problems. You start to realize that your strengths in one season of life can easily be your downfall in the next season of life, but you need to fight the real enemy. Here's a clue: it isn't your spouse. If you believe in God, you must believe in the evil God came to redeem us from, and that evil appears from the devil himself and he loves seeing me squirm over things like work schedules and my husband cooking differently than me, because when bigger issues arise, he thinks he will have a foothold. So if you're like me, or you're even like my strong husband, realize that quality time together—as short as it can be—is a choice, despite what life throws at you.

My King, we are so selfish. We thought we'd marry this wonderful spouse who pursues You perfectly and leads or helps us out of that faithfulness, but we see a lot about our spouse that hurts us, distracts us from You, or fails us... it can be discouraging and confusing, because marriage was supposed to look like You, this perfect God, to the church. This (future) marriage isn't perfect, and we know it never will be. I pray that we can find ways to grow as a selfless spouse anyway, because You make beauty out of broken things. Even the strongest, most Godly marriages will never be perfect, like You, but You can shine brightly to this world through those marriages that seek You first.

Amen/so be it.

9 ❧ Family

*Let people in, even into the places that are not your proudest. That way,
there is no doubt who you are, who you've been, and who you want to
be. When there is no doubt of that, they <u>fully</u> enjoy the <u>full</u> person. Our
loved ones or our very self could be gone today, whether we are careful
or not, 'good' or not, saved or not, known well or not. Let people in.*

YOU LOVE THEM AND hate them. You can't choose blood family, but you
can choose family in other ways. Most of us have crazy uncles, smoochy
aunts, and grandmas who love baking cookies, and it all doubles when we
marry. Preston and I? Total, we both have younger brothers named Nathan,
ironically, and I have two sisters (one older and younger). I have one angel
brother because he died from Sudden Infant Death Syndrome (SIDS) in
1999. We all as siblings and siblings-in-law are very close in age. We have a
few grandmas, only one grandpa still living (rest in peace, Chuck), a great
grandparent, and a few aunts and uncles between us. We know Preston's
mom and her husband as well as my parents, and we have plenty of family we
still haven't met yet, like cousins three times removed, whatever that means!
It's more than a lot of people can say, but even if your (future) spouse has one
single parent living and a dog, that's a family you'll inherit when you marry,
and your spouse will "marry" your family also.

Marrying the Family

For anyone who wants to marry, you may know that for better or worse, you
marry the family too. As a newly married couple, you'll be your own new
family, even without children, but you still likely will see your in-laws or
interact with them. So, get to know your spouse's family, especially before

you marry, because you will want to know what you're walking into. You don't get to choose them, but you chose your spouse, so honor them by trying to get to know their family.

You may decide as a new family that some family members should be distanced from you. My dad, when I was a baby, decided he should keep our family at a distance from his mother. His reasons I support because as a child he wasn't well taken care of—not by his mother anyway. That's putting it lightly.

You may need to know what your spouse's childhood was like, because in marriage, things tend to reveal themselves. My husband lost his dad to a tragic accident before I could meet him, so I don't get to have a father-in-law, except sort of through his mom's husband. As Preston's wife, I've gotten to see him walk through healing, and I've gotten to see how he interacts with father-like figures. Knowing these things really matter. Knowing things— such as how your spouse deals with loss, knowing that perhaps your in-laws don't come around to visit unless it's the holidays, and knowing virtually anything familial— can spare you some arguments and heartache down the line, especially when you as a couple encounter your own trials.

Your Future Family

I acknowledge that some of you are engaged and may already have children, either with your future spouse or with someone else, but this section could still come as an encouragement; however, this section is primarily for those who do not yet have children.

As I write this, I am not pregnant. In May 2016, my husband and I started trying to conceive. I've heard it said "if you aren't trying *not* to conceive, then you're trying to conceive," so you newly marrieds, if you don't want children right away, decide how you will avoid it (birth control pills, tracking ovulation through kits or basal body temperatures, or any other form of protection).

On a side note, for those not sure if they want children right away, I'd recommend at least 2 years being just spouses, maybe even five. Think of it this way: women can healthily bear children before about age 40, and if you take care of yourself, you can take care of children much later in life than you expect, while still enjoying it, if becoming pregnant doesn't happen right away. Likely, your children will live with you until about age 18-23, so even if you got married mid-20s, at age 40 you'll be at the peak of your life and still have decades before you start to *feel* old. Even if you had a child at age 30, you'll be in your mid- to late-40s when they move out.

This is a very general example, but in the end, God decides when you have children, even if you are using contraceptives. And trust me, my husband and I, since starting the conception journey, have done everything short of in-vitro procedures and artificial insemination and God has not given us a child yet. It is out of our hands. As my friend Taylor once said, "it is practically a miracle women get pregnant." Of course, when you are trying actively to conceive, it can seem as though a miracle is needed only for you, because most women around you are getting pregnant, right?

Well, I think it's just a mental thing. It's like looking for a new car... before knowing the kind you want, you may not notice a specific kind. But once you choose a make and model of car, or choose that you want a baby now, you see it popping up everywhere. It's how our brains were designed.

For those newly married and trying to conceive, I'd like to talk to you. I don't have a lot of *experience* with conception obviously, but I have learned a lot through reading, prayer, and conversations with others about this. I'd like to offer you some tips and challenges, because you will need tips and will face challenges at some point.

Challenges. If you're not sure what challenges you could have getting pregnant, let me share what possible issues could arise. I cannot share every resolution to these issues because my lack of experience does not make me that informed, and I cannot possibly know every issue known to man, but in the next sections I will share what I know to the best of my knowledge.

Now, a smaller challenge you will face are the dreadful waiting periods as you wait for symptoms and positive tests. There might be severe symptoms if you are early pregnant like morning sickness (at any time of day), nausea, backaches and headaches—and ladies there are many more. A challenge I faced in these last couple months is having symptoms I've never had before, even though I wasn't pregnant at all. It's like I wanted it so badly, my body mimicked symptoms just to spite me. Plus, period symptoms are annoyingly similar to pregnancy symptoms in many cases.

Some of you will face having no symptoms, yet still could be pregnant, so the waiting will be difficult, and the positive test might be a surprise.

Usually missing a period (if you are regular) is the first sign of pregnancy. I am very irregular, which is basically anything not consistent or typical: periods longer than 7 days, cycles longer than 35 days or so, or missing periods often. That's likely *why* we haven't conceived yet, but we don't know the *how* of that *why*. The doctor said essentially that it sometimes "just happens" to some women, and my blood test showed everything as "normal." It's possible something is affecting us on my husband's side too, but ultimately, God can open a barren womb or keep a fertile one closed. It is His will we seek, even when it hurts deeply and the wait is long.

Some more serious challenges are: ovarian cysts or uterine fibroids (talk with your doctor to check), males being sterile and women being barren, and physical incapability to conceive, especially if you have had abortions before. You'll have to closely monitor medicine, food, and alcohol intake, even before confirmed pregnancy. But despite the risks and annoying symptoms, taking care of yourself physically, emotionally, and spiritually can ensure the healthiest season of trying, and the healthiest pregnancy possible. This modern age not only provides advanced medical options, but God still has the power to open your womb like He did in biblical times (Job 3, Job 10, Isaiah 44, Jeremiah 1, *et al*).

Let's not forget the challenge of having to face what you call "failure" in trying to conceive by getting the same advice from people over and over, even if people mean well. Things like *if you stop stressing, you'll conceive* can really humble you and frustrate you all at once. It's like you'll never quite feel stress-free enough to conceive correctly...but it is out of our hands regardless! Sure, stress less. They are right that stress affects healthy conception. It causes unnecessary pain and could hurt your health, but know that *it isn't your fault*—yes, even if you are "infertile."

Mothers To-Be. As a young woman, I had always dreamt of surprising my husband over a nice dinner with a positive pregnancy (the first try of course), and us sitting down over dessert to plan what we would buy for the baby. But it hasn't happened that way. In fact, it was my husband that decided we would start trying, after me begging him for months, and he has known about all of my countless negative pregnancy tests, and about every symptom I've faced. When I am pregnant, he will not be surprised, but that does not mean he will not be overjoyed, relieved, and excited.

Invite your husband into this process, even if you dream like I did to keep it a secret and floor him with the news. You might be surprised that he wants to be involved, and that you'll need him. You may decide as a couple to invite others in too, at least for prayer and advice. Close friends, your parents, other family members or coworkers, especially current mothers, can offer comforting assurances, helpful advice, and an open ear. I didn't expect to tell anyone about us trying—before a positive pregnancy test at least—but I've told several friends, and even my own parents. I was so relieved to ask my mom, and close female friends, about their experiences. I originally didn't want to even tell anyone, because I wanted to tell everyone as a surprise (and I was expecting it'd be after a few weeks of trying, but boy was I wrong).

It's more than okay to find ovulation predictor kits, and to pay attention to your body, but make sure that you pray constantly (1 Thessalonians 5:16–8). Also, don't forget not to overanalyze every little twitch and temperature change, because it can easily switch over from moderate diligence to overstress. I believe God can and will bless Godly people with children at the right time, even without ovulation predictor kits. It can be painful to believe God wants you to marry then have children, but to still see unwed women conceiving, and discount it as God not seeing your faithfulness. Maybe God can use their child too! Maybe you can still celebrate with that woman as she becomes a mother! Jesus Christ's own mother wasn't yet married when the Holy Spirit gave her the Savior, so God can use anything.

I know that watching women become pregnant who *don't* want a child can break your heart. That's why fostering and adopting is so essential! Maybe that can be you—or us—even if you *do* conceive naturally. Know that even if you "pray circles" (Batterson, *The Circle Maker*) around starting a family, it can feel like you're praying more than *that other person*, but God isn't punishing you. As my friend Jason says in his song *Pray it Through*, "… don't give up until the answer's there with your breakthrough. Jesus said to pray so that your heart will be filled with joy. Pray it through."

Fathers To-Be. Men, pray for your wives and future children, even before you know she has conceived. As a leader of your household, I am asking you to pray for, and *with*, your wife. It will be so comforting to hear your open heart whispered aloud to God on her behalf and on behalf of your (future) child. Even as we knew I was not pregnant (and still am not), we prayed for God's will in the timing of giving us a child, and we thanked God for the child He will give us one day. Trust me, it's key to peace. Our prayers sound like this: "Lord, thank You for this child that You have planned for us. We look forward to being pregnant." Sometimes I pray "Lord, please, I beg you, I don't care if I throw up due to morning sickness, I want a baby now!" He still hears even those kinds of prayers and probably smiles at me, like a father would at their child begging for a new toy that the father has hiding behind his back in secret.

I talked to my husband about what advice he would give to you men, and he said that this is a serious process. "Be patient and loving to your wife as she goes through body changes (even when she is not pregnant), and when she needs emotional support." Preston and I want you to know that your manhood, and your worth in God, is by no means diminished by this being a *long* process. Long to us may not be that long ultimately—not to God, and not to us in hindsight, hopefully. If in a year of trying you do not conceive, of course consult a doctor, both of you, but there is no fault or blame. Nobody chooses infertility.

Spouse Over Children

Both men and women, I urge you whenever you have children to never let them become priority over your spouse.

I hear too often that having children means you can't really travel anymore, and I refuse to let that be true when I have children! I want my children to see the world *with us!* Having children surely changes your life and makes it more difficult to plan vacations, and you certainly have to save more money and bring more food and other things, but it comes down to the choice: will you try? Is it worth the memories you'd make? Just commit to discuss the changes in budget, emotions, and your household because of your growing family. This is just one way people forfeit living. Children should—despite it taking more effort—be a part of your memories, not be the reason you stop making some.

I know children need their parents to guide them. They need a mother's tender nurturing and a father's strong and steady hands to guide the way for them, but mothers and fathers need each other too. That never changes.

The whole family, first and foremost, needs God. Remember earlier? First God, then spouse, then children.

Money

When we hear "I'm on a budget," we tend to think people don't have a lot of money. But that phrase really just means, "I didn't *plan or allot* this money for this item/event." I bring up budgets because even if you become a millionaire, I'd even say *especially* if, then you should know where your money is going. That's all a budget is. It can actually be a freeing thing, not a restrictive thing.

Budgets, especially when they are created and monitored *together* and *regularly*, can reveal how much income you have coming *in* and how much you can *spend* on bills, savings, giving away, and yes, fun money for your date nights and family nights. I know it's counterintuitive, but even plan for spontaneity. Why? Because being spontaneous too often without budgeting for it could mean you're spending more than you're earning. You don't want to come back from a spontaneous day trip without enough money for the mortgage.

Another essential thing to budget for, especially if you want to live debt-free and credit-card-free like my husband and I, is the emergency fund, coined from Dave Ramsey and his daughter Rachel Cruze. It isn't meant to be your *savings account*, but a virtually untouchable cash fund either in another account, another bank, or a personal safe of at least three to six months of expenses. This fund is **only** meant for emergencies, like all your vehicles get totaled, or someone dies, or someone needs ongoing medical treatments. It might take years to save up for, but start with a baby fund of maybe one thousand dollars, and add to it every month! This is currently what we are planning for next, since we got rid of the car payment!

If you don't use credit cards and you don't make payments on things like furniture (crazy!) or a car (yes, there is a way to pay cash and not make payments), you can use what *would have* been a monthly payment and stash it away in the emergency fund! The only debt my husband and I have is:

+ **Our house.** We have a thirty year mortgage and we thankfully didn't have a down payment since we went through the VA (Veteran

Affairs) loan, but if you decide on a fifteen year fixed rate mortgage, imagine what kind of freedom you can have paying off way sooner and without all that interest at the backend!

o   This kind of debt is more of an *investment*, but you need to be prepared and financially able to commit to this. You don't *need* a house the second you get married if you are not able to afford 25% (or less) of your take-home pay on a mortgage.

o   You can buy a house *without* credit at all! The process involves **manual underwriting.** Dave Ramsey and Rachel Cruze are my go-to experts on all things finance.

We just paid his vehicle off and bought a used (and still reliable) vehicle for him in cold hard cash, but as of September 2017 and earlier, we had a stupid car payment. Most families do. Now we can really get serious about our emergency fund. Sometimes the peace of driving a used car that's all paid for is way worth not having to pay for a bright and shiny car for years and years until it's lost its value. Imagine what $500 a month saved could do!

Budgeting isn't just recording how much you spend after the fact; it is setting a limit on every dollar you earn *before* you spend it. God gave us all we own, so this is part of smart stewardship. The key is making sure you spend less than you make—at all costs. Sometimes, you have to sacrifice every once in a while, but sacrificing one more vacation a year, or five less coffees a month, are far worth avoiding having to sacrifice peace of mind.

Make a date out of it. Set a time each month to spend an hour or so looking over if you've kept your budget and how you need to adjust it next time. Maybe you retreat to a nice place (that doesn't break the bank) and you enjoy your spouse's company as you balance the books, or you are just discussing it over a nice meal at home.

However you do it, budget regularly and budget together.

My husband, between the two of us, is definitely the bookkeeper. I am not the girl who overspends and puts my marriage in debt because I buy too many shoes. In fact, I am very good at finding deals, being frugal, and respecting our budget, but my husband by far never exceeds the budget. As the man, he really feels in charge of our finances when he manages the books. That does not mean, however, that we don't discuss our budget and expenses. We both made the choice in marriage to join bank accounts and to at least monthly evaluate our finances.

He *earns* most of our money, I figure out how to *stretch and save* a lot of it! Being economical isn't always earning two full-time incomes, but complementing each other's strengths and weaknesses. It doesn't mean we have "less money" in the bank either; it just means being more patient to "get rich." In fact, sometimes having one spouse "stay at home" makes for a cleaner house, leaves more attention for the children, and gives you even less expenses (like gas money to get to work, or the cost of hiring a sitter or nanny).

Even if it is illogical or less convenient, I let my husband manage the books. Even though I could just as easily do it, he is the one to get online to pay the mortgage and bills. One day, we found a couple of relatively small, but mysterious, charges on our bank statement. Per our research of the website and phone number next to those charges, we believed they were fraudulent charges. It had not yet been resolved because my husband insisted he would take care of it. He was at work from 8a.m. until 6p.m. with a short half hour break, and two fifteen minute breaks; none of those times were adequate enough to resolve the issue. All the while, I was at home with a much more flexible schedule, since I was not working full time and could move errands and chores around, but he didn't want me to handle it.

Does it bother me that if I had called it might have been resolved by now? Yes. Do I see him resolving this later as impractical, inconvenient, and unnecessarily delayed? Sure. But I also know how esteeming this task is for him, and how relieved he will be to have conquered this issue for us. Almost everything in marriage involves sacrificing what we want. I just want our $35 back. Even if my husband did everything he can and we *didn't* get the money back, and maybe even didn't confirm that our bank information was safe, then I still need to give this task to him. In the end, "life happens," as my husband would say. Money can be stressful, but most men I know want the burden of carrying that and resolving that stress. Be sure, money is more stressful if you aren't on the same page with your spouse about it.

Holy One, both of us as (future) spouses have this family that we marry also, and that family can and will influence how we resolve problems, discipline our children, work through trials, and celebrate victories. Family can be both a source of heartache and a source of joy. They can support you, but fail you so quickly. I pray protection over marriages that have unhealthy family dynamics (like abuse of any kinds, of or impersonal interactions with each other, or anything of that sort). Those dynamics find a way of creeping into marriages like moldy food in the fridge—we forget it's there, but we brought it with us. Help our marriages to become a new family, one that desires to seek You in all it accomplishes.

Amen/so be it.

10 ✿ Long Distance

If you want to skip to the end of the story without going through the slow, confusing, and climactic parts, you can't blame the Author for the story not making sense. Sometimes going through the chapters (although it takes longer) will turn the story into something far greater than an easy and predictable life.

 MAGINE YOU HAVE MET the most wonderful future spouse. I am not proposing *love* at first sight is true; *attraction* at first sight (through chosen pursuit of that person) becomes love. Whatever you believe, you have found that person, "the one" perhaps, which I have addressed earlier. And that person, once awe struck and in love with you, is pulled away into a different state and you are now unwillingly separated. That was my life for about three and a half years.

I need to rewind. I set up the *mentality* of the story a little bit, but let me take you to the *setting*. It was the year 2012 (I cannot remember the month but it was early in the year, possibly February or March). My boyfriend Preston and I were sitting in his car, after he had picked me up from my college classes for the day, and we were at the park closest to my parents' house. (We frequented this park often that year or so, not just because it was close to where I lived, but because it usually allowed us space to talk freely). We stopped by this park for a heavier reason this time: so he could talk to me about something he had been thinking and praying about for a while, longer than I may have realized. He wanted to join the Air Force.

As I reflect on this memory with my husband today, he tells me that most of the reason he talked to me about this decision wasn't just to inform me, but to navigate how I was feeling about the whole situation (a quality I love about him to this day). He wanted to understand how I felt, he wanted to get on the same page with me about our future, and he wanted to clear the air of any chance of receiving a "Dear John" letter.

The way I see it, Preston was somewhere in between the person who *needed* to join the Air Force because he needed a job, and someone who was so passionate about serving his country that he couldn't think of anything else more suitable for this point in his life. You see, my husband was looking for jobs he was overqualified for (in my opinion) and he was not catching anything, but he did enjoy the atmosphere of aircraft and the field of justice. This is why he joined the Security Forces (or Military Police). (Fact: Only a minute percentage of the Air Force, I believe less than 4%, flies planes, and he wasn't in that percentage).

I do not recall most of his conversation with me that evening because my mind went to worry mode. It went to the distractions of how I'd get to and from school (I wasn't exactly driving until age 19, and even when I did, I didn't have a vehicle of my own, and having mommy drive me to college was not preferable, nor an expensive bus ticket). I started dreading the loneliness of not seeing my best friend in person for a very long time, possibly as late as college graduation. I probably even thought so far as to think of him getting deployed to enemy territory and getting killed. That's how I let worry drive me (by "drive me" I mean "drive me insane!").

As we dealt with this new season with weekly fifteen minute phone calls, writing letters a lot, skyping even more, and keeping busy, November 2012 came around. He had finished his Basic Training and Tech School and came home for a few weeks as he transitioned to his station in California. In these few weeks, we took advantage of him coming to get me to and from school so we could spend time together after my classes each day.

Sometime in there my birthday even came around! But before my birthday, November 8th of 2012 to be exact, Preston decided he would pick me up, but in a rental car. He could have just carpooled with my mom to get me. It was a Thursday, but I didn't have Friday classes that year so I thought *okay, maybe we will be taking a drive up North since this is basically my Friday. We like to do that. Maybe he is just wanting to do something we used to do before this military life got started. Or maybe not. In fact, I know he's got something up his sleeve. It won't be a normal Thursday…it can't be. He rented a car for some reason!*

But know this: women are hyper-observant, almost more-so when not in the same state as their man. Some time prior to him coming back to Arizona, as we were skyping, he muted me to call my dad (I know this because I heard my dad answer the phone in the other room; I just couldn't hear what they were saying). Now, really folks, why would your boyfriend call your dad except for one thing? So, this particular Thursday when he picked me up in that rental car, I thought *either tonight's the night he would propose, or he wants me to* think *tonight is the night.* Either way, I knew I was going to school in my nicest dress and jacket…just in case!

He picked me up all dressed in his nice dress blues because he also had some military work in town to do, and as I admired (okay, gawked at) how he looked in uniform, we stopped at my sister's and her boyfriend's place, where she and her boyfriend stood. Preston kept me inside the car as they secretly met inside.

Maybe ten minutes later, the three of them came outside and I was already ready to solve this mystery, well, yesterday!

As we departed, her boyfriend said something about enjoying the reindeers, so I at least knew we were going up North, like I originally thought. We drove on a dark and rainy road (yes people, Arizona has rain), listening to K-Love Radio, singing along as we used to do, and we had a huge dinner from Sonic, which I found adorable and unhealthily delicious. We cranked music and ate in our nice clothes some of that greasy goodness (I didn't eat as clean then; college, ya know?). Eventually, we stopped at Sunset Point. (Preston wanted to make it to the gorgeous Mogollon Rim, I found out later, but it was too late, dark, and dangerous to keep going).

I remember it raining so much that when we stopped, we ran out of the vehicle to get under the covered bench area. As I sat on the bench and he kept standing, I heard my sweetheart ramble about someone posting pictures of this place on Facebook. He seemed the most nervous I had ever seen him. As I listened to him talk, he pulled out a piece of paper of his heartfelt thoughts about the journey we had been walking together, and how much he loved me. (Sidenote: we lost this note a year or two later and I cried *hysterically*).

He seemed so romantically focused on reading every word he had written, and even though I sat, he kneeled in front of me and grabbed my hands and I knew…*tonight was the night after all.* As he asked me in so many words (I only remember his eyes) if I would marry him, I said it would be my honor to marry him and we hugged and ran to the vehicle to keep warm and dry. I started contacting family to tell them, but of course, my older sister had half my wedding already planned because she already knew. I think she was living vicariously through me!

Okay, we were finally engaged! We discussed nearly every day how long we should be engaged before we marry. As two children of God, we wanted not only to consider feasibility and convenience in planning time, but how long do we want to fight the battle to abstain from sex. My husband wasn't a virgin, but he had long since been with someone and was going to walk that road with me, which anyone can do if they want to honor God and their future spouse. For those about to marry, I am sure you know how serious this is and how *difficult* this is.

We originally settled on one year from engagement, so November of 2013. But, sometime in the summer, after he went out of state back to his base again and finished some physical training early in the morning, he informed me via phone call that "we won't get married when we want to." Worry mode started again. *Why? Was it me or a situation? What could be happening? Is he getting deployed?*

"I am getting deployed," he uttered, as he somehow read my thoughts.

We had to regroup. Deployment meant he would be out of the country, and it meant we had a lot to discuss; *how long, where, when, and are you going to be on the front lines…?*

Over time we figured it all out, but it added another half year or so to our engagement. We knew instead of November 2013, it'd be February 22, 2014. So not much longer, but now we had to plan our whole wedding apart from each other, and for anyone familiar with the military life, even what they tell you will happen can change, so we wanted to make sure that if we sent invitations, the date wouldn't change last minute, among many other concerns.

My groom made it—the week of the wedding! And unlike November, which is a busy month for our church, rendering our church unavailable the original wedding date, we actually got to marry at Central Christian in February. I won't talk too much about the specifics of our wedding planning. I will just say that your *marriage* is worth more than a *wedding*, but your wedding can be both *wonderful* and *affordable*. You need to *both* make the decisions as well. Will you serve alcohol? What food will you serve? What will be the theme colors? Where will the ceremony and reception be? Who are Maid of Honor and Best Man? Pick a budget and don't budge it (Get it? I just made that up!).

The budget is most important. Money is something that makes more couples divorce or fight, and even if you don't even *threaten* the word "divorce," money issues *always* arise, and money issues cause more divorce than most other issues outside infidelity. I don't care if you are rich or poor, secure or not, both working or not; things happen that require money discussions or adjustments, so start your marriage off right by evaluating what a good budget is for your wedding. Be wise with the *money* God gave you with the *spouse* God gave you. Nothing we have is ours.

Know that the wedding details matter, but none as much as <u>who</u> and <u>why</u> you're marrying.

Back to being long distance. We married and I was able to skip a week of school to have a beautiful honeymoon in—you guessed it—Northern Arizona again, in Flagstaff. But we had to depart again so I could finish school and so he could go back to his California base. We continued to be apart hesitatingly, but with completely no control over it except to visit every couple months until May of 2015, when I graduated. We thought we would be united in Arizona by then, but I went to California to be with my husband until July when we moved back to Arizona together. Now he is in the Reserves.

In marriage, whether long distance or not, you need to constantly share your feelings, desires, and choices—and *pray!* Let God tell you what to do. If you have a choice *not* to be long distance, choose that. If you can make it through the temptations of being away from your spouse (the loneliness, the test to be faithful at all costs, and everything in between) then you can make it through anything. You won't love the situation, but you *choose* to love your spouse enough to endure. Vows are serious oaths, not meager suggestions. You promise thick and thin, so in the thick, stay together. I wonder now if the "thin" is the hard part, like when money is thin in the household? Either way, you better be in it for the long haul, *thick and thin*.

Heavenly Father, some of us are about to be married or are married but are literally separated, maybe due to deployments like Preston and I were. If it is unavoidable, make these marriages find ways to withstand temptations, heartache, and loneliness. You are the most Creative being as Creator, so making memories while way-too-many-miles apart is easy for You. It is not easy for us... we want physical touch and just to be around the person we love 2nd to You, but we sometimes hit walls as to how.

If couples have the choice not to live long distance, make it so. For whatever reason they desire it, outside of mandatory trips they cannot take together for work or whatever else, we aren't meant to be without each other. Give us strength as we navigate this difficult way of living.

Amen/so be it.

11 ❀ Divorce

Love really isn't about deserving it; it reaches its
deepest impact when it is least earned.

TRUTH HURTS, NOT JUST to the one who hears it; the one giving the
truth may experience no change to the person who hears it. However,
I am a firm believer that truth is always necessary to hear and discuss, and
is often controversial. This is one of those things that need to be talked
about, because the world will take truth and either make it a gray issue, or
will completely misuse and abuse that truth as an unmerited freedom, e.g.
getting divorced because you "can" is a truth but it doesn't mean it should
happen for no good reason.

Allow me to elaborate. Think for a second of someone you know who
has gotten a divorce, or even just legally separated. Maybe it was your
parents. Maybe you have already gone through one or are currently. I am
sure that all of my readers know at least one divorce mess. Even in the
biblically permitted divorce situations, it is still messy. It is so sad that I
have such confidence in that high rate of divorce experiences. Most people,
when I was in school, were surprised my parents were still together because
most of them were in a family of divorced parents. There was a time when
divorce was unheard of. Now divorce is an expectation, a welcomed option,
a way out of discomfort. It's practically a wedding vow! "If we ever fall out
of love, we can divorce."

I purposefully put this section at the end of the book because no matter
what, divorce is an end to something. Even when divorce is completely valid,
it is an end to marriage, and usually an end to stability emotionally and
financially. Sometimes it is freeing, especially if the divorce was amicable
and biblical, but the duration and intensity of pain that comes from ending

something that you thought was going to endure is inevitably present—it may be for a long time. Separating "one flesh" (Genesis 2:24, Ephesians 5:31) is always agonizing.

Before I go on too much about my own thoughts, let's look at scripture.

Matthew 5 and 19, Mark 10, and Luke 16 talk about divorce being unlawful in any instance *except* "sexual immorality." This was being discussed because Pharisees wanted (not just in this opportunity) to catch Jesus in a tricky question and stumble over His words, or to contradict Himself. Unfailingly though, Jesus never falls into their traps. Having God communicate to Him (Jesus) comes in handy. He knows their intention to confuse His words or to muddle up a truth.

God hates divorce because God has designed man and woman to be complementary in love and service to each other, to be the example of God and the church. Divorce shows people that God separates from His church—but He doesn't! He *could*, because we fail Him, but He loves us despite the Church, His bride, sinning against Him, being unfaithful to Him. I think the "being one" thing is why, in my long distance years with my husband, I could literally feel my heart being pulled away from my husband when he would drive to the airport to depart—way more than when we were not married.

In the case of adultery, God does not *command* us to divorce. But, He gives us the exception, the option, the permission, because adultery does defile marriage and already has begun the destruction. There is not (as far as my few times going through the whole Bible has taught me) any scripture saying "If a man is physically abusive, you may divorce." When someone marries someone who is already very abusive, it is hard to say, on a biblical standpoint, "yeah, go ahead end it, even though you probably shouldn't have married at all." However, in no way does God commanding husbands to love their wives as Christ loves the church leave room for abuse. Divorce seems justifiable there! Especially if you have children in danger. I am not naïve enough to assume that someone knew their spouse would abuse them. Nobody asks for that.

This also goes for an unbelieving spouse, because being unequally yoked not only can be a temptation to lead you away from God, but can leave you at risk of *irreparable* problems—the kinds worse than the problems you'll have if equally yoked. If you can avoid marriage with that person altogether, it's better all around. But don't think, *oh, maybe if we still live together unmarried*... No, no, no... it can still be toxic or dangerous.

I know at least a couple of strong marriages that had a past of abuse or infidelity, and they have been restored and have stayed married. When you allow God into the situation, anything can be restored if you want it to. This is why marriage should be chosen seriously and kept committedly, and if necessary, divorce is *permitted* but only if it is prayerfully necessary.

Rule of thumb: If you enter marriage thinking divorce should or will happen, I'd probably not marry that person. Divorce is a choice made when something like abuse and sexual immorality permits it; it isn't (or shouldn't be) planned. If either of those issues are happening *before* marriage, don't get married. Don't think marriage will "fix" that person.

I would say that if you marry someone who is abusing you in *any* way—physically, emotionally, or through neglect—there will be patterns in dating and engagement that will give you the clues. I don't think many people are unaware of being abused, but perhaps decide it's worth overlooking because *nobody else notices me* or *maybe they will change*. Even if he (or she) is the only one noticing you, it doesn't mean you should marry them. It doesn't mean someone more suitable can't notice you later in life. And if anyone changes, it isn't a guarantee marriage will provide that—not without supernatural or therapeutic intervention.

The same thing goes for dangerous drug or alcohol abuse; if it is putting that person, yourself, or your children in danger, that is a form of neglect and abuse. That is why premarital counseling and thoughtful prayer is so important before marriage. It reveals areas that need to be addressed. You do not want to be in a situation where you separate what God has meant to be together. It's better to not even enter courtship or engagement—or marriage—at all. Like I said earlier, valid or not, divorce is always costly.

In general, if you are considering divorce, think about what it would cost you financially and emotionally. Are you divorcing because you fight a lot? Is that reason enough? Did you marry that person expecting not to ever fight again? Divorce is a very serious choice people make, and one of the biggest reasons is having money issues—not necessarily having too little money, but not making good *choices* with money, or not *agreeing* on money matters. Get to know your future spouse's money language, something a lot of premarital classes should go through.

Love is more than how you feel. Yes, you'll certainly feel when you love; it'd be silly not to. In fact, "the opposite of love", as is famously quoted, "is not hate but indifference" (Elie Wiesel), which to me says love contains many emotions and feelings. That does not mean, however, that because I don't *feel* love around the clock that I don't *have* love, or that I have tripped over a rock and have "fallen out of love." Falling out of love is a myth. It doesn't *feel* like it did before your husband stopped praying with you, or before the constant fighting. Feelings fluctuate—for me almost every hour—but I love my husband even when he isn't lovable, even when I don't *like* him.

Disappearing "love feelings" happen when we get hurt, when we are apart, when we are working on projects too long, when we are battling addiction, and so on. You won't always feel good inside. Relationships are not just about feeling something; almost always, they are about *giving* even *when* you don't feel.

Feelings still matter. They help us understand why we perform certain actions or behave a certain way, or why our spouse is behaving a certain way. I try to think of "H.A.L.T." Are you (or your spouse) **h**ungry, **a**ngry, **l**onely, or **t**ired? If so, try to resolve *that issue first,* and it can help you understand how to move forward. Even give your spouse a fair warning "hey, I am in kind of a bad mood, so forgive me if I'm a little snappy today." It can diffuse a potential overreaction later in the day.

Some days, I don't *feel* love toward my husband (maybe I feel frustrated or maybe I feel nothing; it just happens now and again), but I still love him. I am not sure I fell in love; rather, my husband pursued me, like God did, through his choice to love me even when I pushed him away, when I didn't love him yet. After thoughtful prayer, I *decided* I would love this man *because* I was loved, and *because* I was *attracted* to him.

Some people say "I love you, but I'm not *in love* with you." What does that even mean? I think it means you don't *feel* like you love them that much, but you care about them as a person. That is an upsetting reason to end a marriage. Maybe they still love them, like how they *chose to* in the beginning, but have been taught that if the feelings aren't there or aren't good, run.

I am not saying you have to stay together. I don't know the situation you're in. But if you aren't going to be together, I don't think it should be just based on feelings. Those change about 15 times a day for me. They change with seasons. Things will get hard. You'll not always get what you put into the relationship. Marriage, for example, is 100/100, not 50/50, but some days, if I am sick or sad, I'm on closer to 40% or 10% or perhaps even on empty... My husband will still give me 100%, when he's at his best anyway. And when he lacks, I'll compensate back.

There is still a choice. You don't just fall out of love—at least not overnight and not by accident. Your emotions, your *feelings*, just may not be there today. Love is first and foremost a choice, and it has just about every feeling you can imagine within it when it's at its best. Just please, don't leave someone just because you don't "feel it" one day. It's not enough. You will never find someone that will keep you in epinephrine heaven 24/7...and even if you did, love is about more than feeling good.

It's not just about you. It's not just about them either. Marriage, when you both pursue God especially, should constantly *emulate* God with His bride, the church.

Even if you *both* don't feel love, then yes, ask the real questions like.... *did we get together for the right reasons? Is there a reason we feel, or don't feel, this way? Can we find ways to feel "that way" more? How can I better serve, respect, and love you?*

It's your choice, and you may choose to breakup. Your first love may not be your last. They may not be who you marry. Just consider the possibility of loving past that rut of not feeling...and ask these questions *before* you start a marriage!

...how deep would you go for someone? Would you go deep enough to love them, even when they don't love you perfectly, and even when you don't feel it all the time? We say "yeah, of course," but what about when they purposefully hurt you? What if they look too long at that underwear ad? What if they don't like going to church? Vows are said once or twice, but they need to be *enacted* too, every day!

Bob Goff beautifully said this about his wife in his book "Love Does (p.52)":

> "Because of our love for each other, I understand just a little more how God has pursued me in creative and whimsical ways, ways that initially did not get my attention. Nevertheless, He wouldn't stop. That's what love does—it pursues blindly, unflinchingly, and without end. When you

go after something you love, you'll do anything it takes to get it, even if it costs everything."

Sacrificial love has greater rewards than the kind of love people offer only on their good days.

And once you "get" someone, you don't get a free pass to coast. You don't say "I love you" at the wedding then never say it again just because they should "already know it." Obviously you work daily at esteeming, respecting, and honoring your spouse and marriage.

I think the biggest point I can make, since a lot of my readers may already be married, is to not consider divorce—period! Eliminate it from your vocabulary. *Never* threaten your spouse with divorce, even when you want to hurt them because you're angry. You don't want to harbor insecurity and worry in your marriage, especially if you have a problem fighting too much. Divorce is not an escape clause. Escape clauses are in contracts, but that's not what marriage is. Marriage is a *covenant,* and those are unbreakable. At least they should be. Divorce is only an unplanned last resort.

Comforter, you designed marriage to be committed like You are to us, and for it to stay together, but you know sin has broken all good things. If there are brittle marriages on the brink of divorce, supernaturally restore them! If there are marriages that are already broken, provide healing, peace, and provision to the very probable lifestyle changes that occur when marriages end. Give unmarried and engaged people a hope, and eliminate any fear in their heart towards marriage. Too many people have divorced or unmarried parents, and that might make it tempting to never marry. You don't require people get married if they want to always be single, and if that's this reader, give them the blessing of relying totally on You, and to not be swayed into sexual sin. For those ready to marry, give them courage to commit and to never even threaten divorce. Give singles patience as they wait for the right person to pursue them through You. Teach all of us, in all walks of life, in all seasons, to trust You to use even the really difficult and annoying things to benefit our walk with You. A special prayer for those with marriages that ended due to death... it is something we hold our breath for and try not to think about until it happens, but it's a shock every time. Give us comfort as we walk through perhaps the hardest season we have ever had to walk through.

Amen/so be it.

Marriage is kind of paradoxical, because it can be both inconvenient and convenient; it has the thrill of familiarizing yourself with someone day by day, year by year, and yet they seem more new to you all at once; it involves loving to our maximum, and yet somehow loving *past that maximum* as time passes; it brings out our most *vulnerable* sides, which *strengthens* its grip on the two married people. Marriage is worth every loss, celebrates every victory, experiences every emotion, and produces hope. Marriage should look like Jesus and the church: relentlessly loving and telling the truth, and being willing to lay down one's life, even when we fail each other, like we have with God.

Marriage isn't about you, and it isn't *just* about the other person either. It's about God! It's *from* God! Somehow as you love and give sacrificially, it fulfills *you* in the deepest way, and it fulfills your spouse too, of course.

Marriage has a lot more to do with sacrifice than it does with *happiness.*

My husband has sacrificed in many ways, even before we married; he sacrificed by marrying a broke college girl and helping her out financially at times; he sacrificed a romantic relationship with me that he desperately wanted in exchange for my friendship, even if that was all he ever got; he sacrifices his comfort and energy when I drag his introverted self out for dates and to spend time with people; he sacrifices time he could use to sleep or complete projects to spend time with me; these are just the ways I can think of quickly. There are countless more.

I sacrificed the *happiness* of being in a relationship with someone for the *joy* and *strength* of getting to know who *I was* when I graduated high school after that big breakup with Justin; I sacrificed a lot to stay in that long distance relationship with Preston for sake of what I knew would be a wonderful future marriage, even before we got engaged; I sacrifice *my* comfort and energy when he prefers to *stay in* for dates.

We both sacrificed comfort, affection, our original wedding date, and sometimes some peace when we lived long distance; we often even sacrifice down to not having our way when we know we are right, and we sacrifice all selfish thoughts and words for sake of our spouse (again, most of the time). Just get used to sacrifice! Your vows better be <u>lived seriously</u> after they are <u>spoken eloquently</u> at your wedding . . . and when you don't succeed at living them out too well one day, make sure to resolve issues, forgive each other, and pray with and for each other.

After you read your vows the first time, and if you renew them later on, live them out in your marriage every day. Know that "God will not *prevent* us from what He will *perfect* us through" (Paul David Tripp, The Art of Marriage).

If I were single, I'd probably have a lot less money but would "do" a lot more, because I am an extrovert who seriously cannot get enough experiences and time with people. Married to an introvert, I sacrifice a LOT, as does my husband as an introvert married to an extrovert. If I were single I'd probably buy more clothes, and I would most definitely not have a house of my own yet. I wouldn't really need one. A small apartment would do so I could just work to save money so I could try new places, foods, and experiences with people all over again!

Being married, I make *different* sacrifices than if I was single, maybe even *more* sacrifices, but I also have gained things I would not have gained single. **There are benefits to both stages in life.** I chose intentionally to move into marriage knowing most of these things. One thing marriage has taught me, though, is just how selfish I am! So I try to shape my life around being a Godly wife, around being as *selfless* as I can.

Making sure my husband has a welcoming and clean home is important to me. Making sure he eats well without having to make most of the meals after a long work week is a pleasure for me. He earns most of what we have financially. He works hard for it. Finances are an area I can never give much of on my own, so I dedicate myself to be generous in time, effort, affection, listening, and helping as I can. Marriage requires intentional work, and you just might get some wonderful things back if your spouse treats it the same way. Mine does.

My love for Preston is exponentially deepened by our mutual oneness in God, being **equally yoked** spiritually. We both want a family to steward and love, and we manage money and time in a way that complements each other's needs and strengths. I am confident every year of marriage will teach me something new. Sure, dating does that. Living with someone does that. But marriage in itself is something more priceless and sacred than some people believe it is.

Everything good I have is from God, including my husband and this thing we call marriage! I steward them as carefully as I do dollars and minutes. Marriage isn't a ball and chain, or a prison cell, or a means to selfish ends. Marriage to us is a powerful vehicle for changing ourselves, not our spouse—but I promise it will change them too. Just remember, any victory will come with a preceding battle, and it is God supplying those victories. It is also God providing some of those battles; it's worth it, every ounce of discomfort and pain, because discomfort brings a need to yield to God, and pain makes us thankful for the better times.

In the end, just be the kind of spouse you want *your spouse* to be, because greater the chances are that they will become the same for you. We can't change our spouse; God changes our spouse—*and us too*. When you love even their most unlovable parts, forgive their worst mistakes, desire them and fulfill them sexually, and pray for them diligently, even when they aren't doing all that for you yet, they won't want to seek someone else. (If they still seek someone else, then there is something deeper going on and it isn't your fault). Your marriage will be so intimate, sweet, strong, and original. It isn't a promise of a flawless marriage, or that your spouse won't fail you, but it will provide a marriage that looks like Christ to the church—never giving up, always loving and forgiving, shining brighter as time goes on, defying the odds, making no logical sense, and supernaturally thriving through the battles— *and the victories.*

Glossary

Covenant: A solemn oath.

Discernment: The ability to judge well.

Discipleship: A disciple is a student or follower of someone—in this case, of Christ. As such, they spend time with and study about Him. It's a really Christianese way of saying you follow God.

Equally Yoked: A yoke is a wooden bar that joins two oxen to each other and to the burden they pull. An "unequally yoked" team has one stronger ox and one weaker, or one taller and one shorter. The weaker or shorter ox would walk more slowly than the taller, stronger one, causing the load to go around in circles. When oxen are unequally yoked, they cannot perform the task set before them. Instead of working together, they are at odds with one another. Spiritually, this is similar to one praying and the other doesn't; one spends time with God, and the other doesn't; one believes marriage is a covenant by God and one believes it is a contract with an escape clause; need I go on?

Eustress: Moderate or normal psychological stress interpreted as being beneficial for the experiencer. Imagine planning a trip or general motivation to clean out the garage.

First-fruits: This refers to the first (and best) offerings given to God in sacrifice in Old Testament scripture. In modern times, it is the first *offering* or *tithe* (meaning ten percent) of our income.

Manual Underwriting: A process (typically for people with no credit) where a Federal Housing Administrator (FHA) underwriter does the work a traditional and automatic underwriting process would entail.

Millennial: Although there seems to be overlapping opinions and disagreements as to what age group belongs in this category, it is generally accepted that anyone born between 1982 and 2004 is a millennial.

Bibliography

Introduction

Jayna Richardson. (2017, March 8). Equally Yoked—God's Perfect Plan: Though obedience to God can be difficult, it's always worth it. Retrieved from http://www.familylife.com/articles/topics/marriage/getting-married/choosing-a-spouse/equally-yoked-gods-perfect-plan

Chapter 1, Victory Implies Battle

Family Life. (2017, March 1). Art of Marriage. Retrieved from the class and http://www.familylife.com/theartofmarriage

Chapter 2, Dating

Sarah Maxwell. (2016, December 6). Engaged and Living Together. Retrieved from https://snmwifesavedsinger.wordpress.com/2016/12/06/engaged-and-living-together/

Chapter 3, Purity

Resources for freedom from porn addiction:

Bethany Baird. (2017, February 26). Retrieved from https://www.girldefined.com/finding-freedom-addiction-porn

Davenport, M., Hunt, J., (Producers), & Hunt, J. (Director). (February 25, 2017). *Addicted to Porn: Chasing the Cardboard Butterfly* [Motion Picture]. USA: Gravitas Ventures.

Fight the New Drug. (2017, February 7). Retrieved from http:// fightthenewdrug.org/get-the-facts/

Kristen Clark. (2015, September 16). Retrieved from https://www. girldefined.com/porn-christian-girl-needs-to-know

Kristen Clark. (2017, June 16). Retrieved from https://www.girldefined. com/why-i-chose-to-save-sex-for-marriage

Chapter 5, Intimacy

Chapman, G. (1995). *The 5 Love Languages: The Secret to Love That Lasts.* Chicago, IL: Moody Publishers. Retrieved from http:// www.5lovelanguages.com/

Jernigan, C. (Pastor). (2016, November 20). Central Christian Church. *Hope in the Home.* Video Podcast retrieved from https://media. centralaz.com/2016/11/20/hope-in-the-home-2/

The Myers and Briggs Foundation. (2016, December 29). Retrieved from https://www.16personalities.com/free-personality-test

16 Personalities. (2016, December 29). Retrieved from http://www. myersbriggs.org/my-mbti-personality-type/mbti-basics/

Sarah Maxwell. (2016, October 31). As an Extrovert. Retrieved from https:// snmwifesavedsinger.wordpress.com/2016/10/31/as-an-extrovert/

Chapter 7, Prayer

Omartian, S. (1997). *The Power of a Praying Wife (Military Edition).* Eugene, OR: Harvest House Publishers.

Chapter 8, What About Me?

Alcorn, R. (2011). *Managing God's Money: A Biblical Guide.* Carol Stream, IL: Tyndale House Publishers.

Two budget sheets from Dave Ramsey:
Dave Ramsey. (2017, February 11). Retrieved from
1. **Quick-start Budget:**
   https://cdn.ramseysolutions.net/media/pdf/forms/fpu_qbudget.pdf

2. **Monthly Cash-flow Plan:**
   http://cdn.tidyforms.com/Download/Files/monthly-cash-flow-plan.pdf

Chapter 9, Family

Batterson, M. (2011). *The Circle Maker: Praying Circles Around Your Biggest Dreams and Greatest Fears.* Grand Rapids, MI: Zondervan Publishing.

Chapter 11, Divorce

Goff, B. (2012). *Love Does.* Nashville, TN: Thomas Nelson, page 52.

Related Resources

Chapman, G. (2012). *The 4 Seasons of Marriage: Secrets to a Lasting Marriage.* Carol Stream, IL: Tyndale House Publishers.

Cunningham, T., Smalley, Dr. G. (2008). *The Language of Sex: Experiencing the Beauty of Sexual Intimacy.* Ada, MI: Revell, Baker Publishing Group.

Dillow, J., Dillow, L., Pintus, P., Pintus, L. (2015). *Intimacy Ignited: Discover the Fun and Freedom of God-Centered Sex.* Carol Stream, IL: NavPress.

Feldhahn, S. (2004). *For Women Only: What You Need to Know about the Inner Lives of Men.* Danvers, MA: Multnomah Books.

Feldhahn, S. (2006). *For Men Only: A Straightforward Guide to the Inner Lives of Women.* Danvers, MA: Multnomah Books.

Feldhahn, S., Gross, C. (2015). *Through a Man's Eyes: Helping Women Understand the Visual Nature of Men.* Danvers, MA: Multnomah Books.

Jernigan, J. (2015). *Redeeming Pleasure: How the Pursuit of Pleasure Mirrors Our Hunger for God.* Brentwood, TN: Worthy Publishing.

Kelly [no last name given]. (2017, June 14). 35 ways to save money. Retrieved from http://www.viewalongtheway.com/2014/02/30_ways_to_save_money/

Smith, J. (2015). *The Unveiled Wife: Embracing Intimacy with God and Your Husband.* Carol Stream, IL: Tyndale Momentum.

Wheat, Ed M.D. (Author), Wheat, G., Rainey (Author), D. (Foreword). (2010). *Intended for Pleasure: Sex Technique and Sexual Fulfillment in Christian Marriage.* Ada, MI: Revell, Baker Publishing Group.

Reader's Guide

This is a guide for between spouses or with other couples. Use these questions as a place to discuss real matters in your own (future) marriages. It will not necessarily resolve problems or replace premarital counseling or classes, but it can be a part. If you are engaged couples, you might have to modify the questions to be relevant and appropriate. These are best discussed as you complete each chapter, or the whole book, as opposed to prior to reading. Each question is labelled with the corresponding chapter.

*Means it could be really sensitive, and requires extra maturity and wisdom if you should discuss this at all.

1. What battles are most prominent in your marriage? (*Victory Implies Battle*)
2. How do you both define dating? How did that look in your preparation for marriage? (*Dating*)
3. *How do you define purity? Do you agree that it isn't just physical? (*Purity*)
4. Do you agree that there isn't really "the one"? (*"The One"*)
5. What are ways you can grow more intimately with God—both as a couple and as individuals? How might this affect your marriage? (*Intimacy*)
6. *Were both of you virgins upon your wedding day? How did that affect your first night together as a married couple? (Or how do you think that will affect it?) (*The Honeymoon*)
7. Do you pray together as a couple? What things/people do you pray most about? (*Prayer*)

8. In what ways can you become less selfish in your marriage? Men: How can you lead better? Women: How can you help/serve better? (*What About Me?*)

9. How have you seen your family dynamics affect your marriage for the positive and/or negative? (*Family*)

10. How many of you have been in a long distance relationship before (even if not with your spouse)? What kinds of challenges did that cause on the relationship? (*Long Distance*)

11. *Who of you have experienced divorce, either personally, with your own parents, or someone else? Was that divorce biblically appropriate? How has that affected your views on marriage and divorce as a couple? (*Divorce*)

About the Author

Sarah is age 24. She has been married since February 22nd, 2014. The life she lives, which has influenced her writing, goes in the order: God, Spouse, everything else. "Everything else" includes her career as a teacher of young children (various ages over the years from birth through age 8), her passion in leading worship with her voice at Central Christian Church in Arizona, and being a foodie! Basically, there isn't a food she won't try as long as it doesn't  move! In May of 2015, Sarah graduated from Arizona State University with a Bachelor's (BAE) in Early Childhood Education/Special Education. Sarah and her husband do not yet have children, but are hoping to very soon. As an extrovert, she tends to be around people often. She dresses as colorfully as she feels she behaves! Sarah is sister to 4 siblings, one of which is in heaven. Her parents have been married since February 9th, 1991. A lot of what she knows about marriage began with growing up in a household where divorce wasn't an option. For more on this author, find her on social media.

Facebook: @SMaxwellAuthor
Instagram: @smaxwell_author_official
Twitter: @SNMAuthor

Printed in the United States
By Bookmasters